Creative Writing Series
— 18 —

D1281858

Cover: Compugraphics by Pierre Bertrand.

Photo by Dr.Y.K. Chang

Luciano Pradal

Chronicles of an Ottawa Chestnut Lover

New York   Ottawa   Toronto

Pradal, Luciano, author
    Chronicles of an Ottawa chestnut lover / Luciano Pradal

(Creative writing series ; 18)
Text mostly in English with some French and Italian.
ISBN 978-1-897493-45-8 (pbk.)

    1. Pradal, Luciano--Anecdotes. 2. Chestnut--Ontario--Ottawa--Anecdotes. 3. Merchants--Ontario--Ottawa--Anecdotes. I. Title. II. Series: Creative writing series ; 18

TX814.2.C48P73 2013   641.3'453   C2013-907392-2

http://www.legaspublishing.com

lpradal@bell.net

LEGAS

P. O. Box 040328   3 Wood Aster Bay   5201 Dufferin Street
Brooklyn, New York Ottawa, Ontario   Toronto, Ontario
USA 11204   K2R 1B3   M3H 5T8

Printed and bound in Canada by Gauvin Press

To the citizens of Ottawa
that encouraged and supported me.
Thank you!

Canadian Forest with Chestnut Groves. Photo: Greg MacG.

Canadian Chestnut Groves. Photo: Greg MacG.

Contents

Introduzione

Nella quieta maestà di Ottawa, gli inverni si inseguono bianchi e freddi, e i giorni a volte sono luminosi, altre volte capricciosi. Se in uno di questi, diciamo dal venerdì alla domenica, vi capita di giungere nella zona del mercato, solitamente affollata di gente del posto e di turisti, un profumo nell'aria prima o poi vi colpisce. Chi tra voi per antica memoria lo riconosce, riandrà col pensiero e i ricordi al proprio luogo di provenienza, forse l'Italia, o la Francia, o altri paesi dell'Europa dell'Est, o altri ancora di questo vasto mondo. Chi invece non ne ha conoscenza, non potrà fare a meno di incuriosirsi. Sono le caldarroste di Luciano, che sanno di inverni natalizi e di calore tra le mani quando le si aprono per gustarle.

Luciano Pradal, veneto per nascita e per parlata, l'inglese e il francese ormai fluenti, è uno dei tanti immigrati italiani giunti in questo paese molti, molti anni fa. Pasticcere, panettiere, operaio, meccanico, da qualche tempo anche guida turistica, ha contribuito assieme a tutti coloro animati da buona volontà, a rendere questo paese ricco, bello e accogliente. L'ho conosciuto un giorno d'inverno, mentre camminavo 'intabarrato' per il freddo, attirato dalla vista di un caldarrostaio intento al suo lavoro tra i fiocchi di neve. Siamo diventati amici.

Il libro che ora avete sottomano, *Cronache di un amante dicaldarroste di Ottawa*, si presenta come una sorta di diario, non cronologico, che raccoglie brevi resoconti di momenti vissuti e amati con chi, davvero tantissimi, si ferma, compra, assaggia, interloquisce. Luciano 'il caldarrostaio', non è più solo lui, ma esiste assieme al bambino che per la prima volta, al tatto di una castagna calda, sorride e sgrana gli occhi per la gioia, o assieme alla coppia di giovani o di anziani che infilano il sacchetto in tasca per poi esprimere un desiderio segreto e intimo, così come si deve fare quando si 'pela' la prima. Tradizioni italiane, conservate e tramandate, preziose, buone.

Nato per gioco, questo è un libro di relazioni e incontri, ricco di aneddoti seri e divertenti, bizzarri e accattivanti, accomunati da una profonda umanità.

All'inizio sono appunti presi veloci per fissare un istante, caturare un'emozione, come da pittore impressionista pronto a cogliere col pennello la carezza della luce. Piccoli foglietti, fazzoletti di carta, il retro di un biglietto da visita, Luciano si serve di tutto per la scrittura di ciò che vuole ricordare. E parla, parla, parla, attira i passanti, ne solletica la voglia, li accompagna alla scoperta, come naturale anfitrione.

Nella quieta Ottawa, Luciano Pradal è ormai diventato un punto di riferimento, davanti a "La Bottega", in pieno mercato. La città ne ha bisogno, sarebbe più vuota e triste senza di lui.

Ci piace immaginare che l'idea del libro abbia preso corpo sotto il pergolato di casa sua, in una giornata di sole, la vista allietata dal giardino e dall'orto ben curati. E' il posto degli ospiti. Luciano, generoso amico, li accoglie. A ben guardare, il libro è un libro d'amore, un tributo alla bellezza e alla sorpresa degli incontri, non di rado 'straordinari', come direbbe l'autore. Sappiate che di questo sono intessute le pagine, di sentimenti ed emozioni. Avvicinatevi allora con garbo e con cura, vi si apre un mondo altrimenti invisibile. Buona lettura a tutti voi.

Con affetto

Paolo Voltolini   Ottawa, 30 ottobre 2013

Introduction

In the quiet majesty of the city of Ottawa, winters follow one another white and cold, and the days at times are brilliant and at others whimsical. If on one of these days, let's say from Friday to Sunday, you happen to arrive at the Market, usually crowded with local people and tourists, sooner or later you will be hit by a peculiar aroma. He who recognizes it, because of old memories, will turn his thoughts and memories to his place of origin, perhaps Italy, or France, or other East European countries, or still others in this vast world. He who does not recognize it cannot help but become curious. It is the aroma of Luciano's roasting chestnuts that have the taste of winters at Christmas time, and the warmth in your hands when you open the chestnut to savour it.

Luciano Pradal, from the Veneto Region by birth and speech, and also fluent in English and French, is one of the many Italian immigrants who arrived in this country many, many years ago. Pastry maker, baker, labourer, mechanic, lately even tourist guide, together with all those people of good will, has contributed in making this country rich, beautiful and welcoming. I met him one winter day as I was walking, all bundled up because of the cold, attracted by the sight of a chestnut roaster absorbed in his work in the falling snow. We became friends.

The book that you have in your hand, *Chronicles of an Ottawa Chestnut Lover,* presents itself as a kind of diary, not a chronological one, that gathers brief tales of moments lived and cherished by those who stop, buy, taste, engage in a conversation. Luciano the "chestnut roaster" is no longer alone but with a child who for the first time upon touching a warm chestnut smiles and opens his eyes wide with joy, or with a couple of young people or older ones who put the bag in their pocket to later satisfy an intimate and secret craving—just like one does when peeling the first chestnut.

Italian traditions, precious, good, preserved and handed down.

Born out of fun, this is a book of acquaintances and encounters, rich in anecdotes that are serious and amusing, whimsical and captivating, sharing a deep sense of humanity. At the beginning they are quick notes taken to capture an instant, an emotion, like an impressionist painter ready to capture with a stroke of his brush the caress of light. Small sheets of paper, paper handkerchiefs, the back of a visiting card. Luciano uses anything to write down what he wants to remember. And he talks, talks, talks, attracts the passersby, instills in them the desire, accompanies them in their discovery, like a natural host.

In the quiet city of Ottawa Luciano Pradal has now become a point of reference, in front of "La Bottega," in the Market. The city needs him, it would be empty and sad without him. We like to think that the idea of the book was born under the pergola of his house, on a sunny day, the sight gladdened by the well cared for garden and vegetable garden. That's the place for guests. Luciano, a generous friend, receives them there. If we look closely, the book is a book of love, a tribute to the beauty and to the surprise of the encounters, often "extraordinary" as the author would say. Know that this is what the pages are filled with, feelings and emotions. Then approach it with courtesy and diligence and an otherwise invisible world will open up for you. Good reading to all of you.

With affection
Paolo Voltolini   Ottawa, October 30, 2013

Author's Preface

Why have I gone through this great experience? Was it a coincidence? Most people says that coincidences do not exist. Things happen because some "forces" make them happen. And here I am selling freshly roasted chestnuts in the ByWard Market in downtown Ottawa. I would have never expected in my life to be here and to do what I am doing.I am convinced that it is not a coincidence. Who should I thank for this great experience?

The list of people that I should thank is too long, but you can get the idea while reading the *Chronicles of an Ottawa Chestnut Lover.* How many people I interacted with and how many people learned the "chestnut culture," and how many people were looking forward to the weekend to come to the ByWard Market to talk to me, to share some moments of their life, or...I don't know...To savour a freshly roasted chestnut.

I am sure that while reading the *Chronicles* you will notice the rationality and the irrationality of human beings. Can these chronicles change this? I don't know. But I do know that this is an every day experience for any one that is in a social contact with people.

I look at these chronicles as facts of life, facts that evolve in front of you and me regardless of whether we want it or not, sometimes unexpectedly, sometimes happy, sometimes.....Well, that's life.

I only hope that these chronicles do something positive to any one that reads them, that shares them, that talks about them, that has a positive dialogue about them.

I hope the young generation will learn something positive from those pages.

Buona lettura!

Luciano

How I became a Castagnaro!

It all started in 2007. Once I retired as a "Stationary Engineer" the door of a new profession opened up, and I became a "tourist guide" for Italians visiting Ottawa.

But that's another story...

In February 2008, I went to Italy to attend the BIT (Biennale Italiana del Turismo) in Milan. There I met Ernesto Milani who made me feel at home by showing me the city, by touring it, by walking everywhere, and, by savouring some roasted chestnuts we bought from a street vendor. I liked the experience and I took some photos.

Back in Ottawa, while chatting with Nino and his son Gianni (John) Frigo, owners of a welding shop in Ottawa's Little Italy, I showed them the photos of the chestnut roaster I had taken in Milan. I actually left a photo with Gianni.

Some time went by. One day, in the Fall of 2009, Gianni called me:

"Luciano, can you smell roasted chestnuts?"

I was surprised.

"Come down and see for yourself!" Gianni added.

I went to the shop and ...there it was ...a *fornella* with some beautiful, freshly roasted chestnuts! I might add that, after tasting them, we found them to be delicious.

Present at the "Tasting Ceremony" was also Joe Calabro the owner of "Pasticceria, gelateria italiana" on Preston Street located not too far from the welding shop on Larch Street.

It was then that we, Gianni, Joe and I, decided to start the business of roasting chestnuts. Gianni built the cart for the *fornella*, which, now that I know how to use it, turns out to be a piece of marvelous engineering. I applied and got the license from the City of Ottawa. Joe called *The Ottawa Citizen*. A reporter came to see us. He was excited, so he wrote a very nice article which appeared in the newspaper. With all this done we were ready to start the "chestnut roasting adventure."

The launching took place in front of "La Pasticceria" and then we repeated it in other places in Little Italy. We had a lot of success. People were interested in the new experience and excited to taste the freshly roasted chestnuts. For many people that was a new experience.

We, the three "business associates," were very interested to really start and improve the business. We took great care to record all the data associated with it, but, as we quickly realized, it was the wrong time of the year. It was the beginning of January 2010 and, as we now know, January is a very slow month for chestnut sales, in fact, for any sales. Gianni and Joe were as disappointed as I was, but all the equipment was there and the business had been launched. I could not step back. I had to fulfill my responsibilities toward the customers, even if there were not that many coming to see me, to encourage me, in front of "La Bottega," at the ByWard Market in downtown Ottawa.

Yes, indeed, I have to say that Joe, Pat, and Rocco Nicastro were very supportive in allowing me to roast chestnuts in front of their shop. I must say that all the City of Ottawa employees and the Fire Department were also very supportive. They helped us to get the licence, and to pass the health and safety inspection. Angelo Filoso, of the Italian Community Center, supported us with the insurance policy required by law.

Another very important source of encouragement came fromPaolo Copelli manager of the ByWard Market. I knew Paolo and I knew his father, but, with the roasted chestnut experience I have learned to further appreciate his qualities, his availability, and his professionalism.

What a fabulous and amazing environment I got into! Incredible! I could not believe it myself! What tremendous support! I could not step back and leave all those people that believed in me and in the "Roasted Chestnut Culture" disappointed.

Here I am now, warmly dressed, in front of "La Bottega," talking to people, socializing, explaining to them the incredible Canadian chestnut culture. Indeed there were 4 billion chestnut trees here on the eastern North American continent. In 1904 a blight destroyed them all. Now the American and the Canadian Chestnut Councils (CCC) are working very hard to bring them back. Last year the CCC planted 400 chestnut trees and this year, 2012, they will plant 3000 more. They hope to have enough volunteers to plant them. (Here is a good deed for those of you reading this article!)

Most people that come to see me to buy or to sample the chestnuts are acquainted with this wonderful nutrient. I said most. Asians, Arabs, Europeans, Africans, know chestnuts, but many Canadians do not.

Well, maybe now you think that I am not humble. I respect your opinion, but I must give credit where credit is due, the Media.

The Media in Ottawa is very supportive in promoting me, my attitude, and my product. After the article for the launching that appeared in *The Ottawa Citizen*, *Le Droit*, the French language newspaper in the Ottawa Region, the *CBC* radio, *CTV* Television also had their say. Lately Bruce Deachman of the *Citizen* wrote an article about me in his series "One in a million." VIA RAIL in their trains' guide, recommended: *"...when in Ottawa go to see Luciano Pradal in the Market and savour the freshly roasted chestnuts."*

At the end of January 2010, I was asked to roast chestnuts for the residents at Villa Marconi, the Italian Senior Citizens Home. I went, and I returned this year only to have the pleasure of seeing these elderly persons savour a "freshly roasted chestnut."

What an incomparable experience!

When I am in the Market, every day, for me, is a great experience. I get to "La Bottega" around 9:00 a.m. I ask Giovanni to make me an espresso that only he can make. Believe me, once you drink *one* of his espressos you are at your best for the whole day!

Back to the chestnuts, now that I have had my espresso.

I start to prepare the wood charcoal. The first passer by:

"How long before they are ready?"

"Come back in half an hour."

"See you then."

A mother and child come by. I take a warm chestnut, I wrap it in a paper towel, I put it in the child's hands and I look at his or her expression. The face lights up and they look at me in marvel because of the warmth that the chestnut has given them.

My experiences and my delight in practising this kind of profession are also intensified by all the passersby that, with great curiosity, reading the signs in the front of the *fornella*, inquire:

"Roasted chestnuts?"

I am quick to respond:

"Yes! Would you like to try one? Free sample!"

While they savour the chestnut I explain what a wonderful food they are. They are good for red blood cells, they lower bad cholesterol, they increase good cholesterol and so on.

Then I ask, especially the ladies, to make a wish as part of the Italian superstition: "the first time you eat something new, you make a wish...for whatever it costs!"

And there they are, with their eyes closed, they make a wish.

A young lady came back to tell me that her wish had come true. She was now pregnant. Wow! I could not believe it myself. Another lady came by:

"Roasted chestnuts?"

"Yes madam."

She sampled one.

Later on she came back with her father, a *friulano*,* in a wheel chair, to sample and buy some freshly roasted chestnuts.

This kind of positive interaction goes on all day while I am enjoying myself roasting chestnuts.

I must say that the people at "La Bottega" are great. From the Nicastro family to all their employees, they ask me if I need an espresso, a cappuccino, a bowl of soup, or one of their fabulous "panini." I usually refuse because, once in a while, I munch on some irresistible chestnuts, and they are, as I soon discovered, "anti-fatigue."

Well, now I say to you, the reader, what I say to my customers:

"Don't believe me. Do some research yourself, and you will see how wonderful this food is. It was called "the bread of the poor, the bread from Heaven." Just have a chestnut with a piece of cheese, keep them in your mouth, savour them, and then wash them down with a sip of read wine. Then, come and tell me what you think."

---

* *friulano*: a man from the Friuli region in Nothern Italy.

Dec. 14th, 2012

I took my granddaughter to school and then I went to "La Bottega" to drop off the chestnuts, the charcoal and other supplies for the day. Then I parked in the City Parking Lot. I walked back to "La Bottega" admiring the different vendors who were also getting ready, hoping for a profitable day.

When I arrived at "La Bottega" I could feel some energy in the air. Everybody was busy. I asked for my usual double espresso and I was served impeccably and quickly!

I went outside. The day announced itself as a beautiful one. It was around 8:30-8:45 a.m.

A distinguished young man arrived with several pairs of pants on his arm. He was looking for Raymond the tailor who had not yet arrived. We socialized and we talked about how priviledged we were to have a "tailor of distinction" like Raymond. On that positive note the gentleman left promising to be back later.

I met him again a few days later.

Again he was carrying pants and a jacket on his arm. He recognized me and he told me that he saw Raymond often.

* * *

I was roasting chestnuts; a man came by:

"How's business?"

"Well," I answered, "I am not really here for the business. I am here to socialize. I am a 'people's person...'"

"Oh!, I didn't notice that..." he said with some sarcastic humor in his voice.

* * *

While roasting the chestnuts I make sure that, if there are some that are not that good I remove them

Later on in the day a man will come to pick them up and feed them to the squirrels on Major Hill Park.

Natural Operation

I am very concerned about the smoke that the *fornella* produces when I start it up. Some of the charcoal is partially wood and this produces some smoke. Most people like the smell. They come around and, with their hands, wave the smoke towards their nostrils saying:

"I love this smell. It reminds me of summer time at the cottage, or roasted chestnuts in England, in Turkey, in Rome..."

I operate the "nature" way but not all people understand that.

Some smoke may enter the buildings in the Market and this is due mostly to the fact that often a building runs on negative static pressure. I have been a "building operator" for thirty five years. I understand how easily a building can run on negative static pressure. All buildings should run on positive static pressure in order to keep the cold air out.

Smoker

The other day it was cold and windy. A person passed by. Out of respect I will call him/her a "It". "It" walked by giving me a certain look that meant that he/she did not like the scent of the smoke. "It" wore no hat or mittens, walked by dragging a little 3-4 years old girl also with no mittens or hat. "It" was puffing heavily on a cigarette!

Back to today.

Panhandlers

A panhandler went by asking my customer, while I was serving him, for some spare change. The customer was upset and answered angrily:

"You are the third person asking me for money in this block!...."

The Chestnut Culture

Education is ignorance's progressive discovery.

There were four billions chestnuts trees on the north eastern American continent but they all died in the 1900s. Most Canadians in this region do not know much about chestnuts and their nutritional value, so here I am "educating" most of my customers.

Ignorance is not a negative. Sometime we ignore things because we were never exposed to them or interacted with them. This is the case of the "chestnut culture," for many people in this region. For those who travel it's a different story, they know, they do not ignore.

Every day I peel a freshly roasted chestnut to show to the customers so they see what a freshly roasted chestnut "looks like" with the caramelized sugars.

Once I see that they are interested, I explain more about them, and tell them how popular they were. The Romans planted chestnuts trees all over the Empire. There are 800.000 hectares of chestnuts in Italy with more than 300 varieties of chestnut trees! The chestnut tree is of the same family as the oak tree. Chestnut trees grow in the mountains and provide a good and healthy food for the people that live, work, and struggle there. The trees produce male and female flowers so one tree can produce chestnuts by pollinating itself!

Photos: Penn Lewis

Chestnuts, in their prickly husk, may grow as one, two, or three.
When there are two the outside shell is harder than the inside; when there are three both sides of the one in the centre are soft.
When I roast them I cut open the exterior lower shell. If I didn't do that the chestnuts would explode.

Difference in Taste

I was serving a couple. A lady came by. She introduced herself. She wanted "that" chestnut she had spotted while I was roasting them.

"That one," she said.

I gave it to her wrapped in a napkin. She peeled it and bit it.

"It's not cooked!" she said.

I stopped talking to the couple and said to her:

"It's o.k. It's cooked, but you have to keep it for a few minutes wrapped in the napkin so that the humidity of the chestnut blends in with the starches and the sugars in the chestnut. See what I am doing here. I put the freshly roasted chestnuts between those two blankets for 5-10 minutes and then they are ready to be tasted, and enjoyed."

Message given!

The Two Blankets

I had not given Renato Marinelli too much credit for the two heat-proof blankets that he made for me and that I use to give the chestnuts that perfect taste. Once I take them from the grill I put them between those two blankets for a few minutes allowing the humidity to blend in with the starches and the sugars. That makes the chestnuts creamier and better tasting.

My Question

It was at the end of the day, when a lady came by. She must have been 55-60 years old.
"Any chestnuts?"
"Sorry, sold out."
"Well," she said, "my mother will have to wait."
I wondered how old her mother was!

"Sitting" and Cupcakes

Another important aspect of my profession as a chestnut roaster is that I have to "sit" husbands, dogs, girlfriends, bicycles, groceries, baby strollers, cars, etc., while people visit the Market or go shopping at "La Bottega."

...*Sitting*.... A lovely couple visit "La Bottega" every Saturday. Upon arrival the husband suggests to his wife what to buy and she goes in. He comes close to me, lights his cigarette, and we socialize. We cover every aspect of society, politics, finances, good food, wines, etc. When his wife comes out with the groceries, we wish each other a good weekend and they go on with their shopping in the market.

... *cupcakes*...On Dec 22nd they came by as usual. They gave me a box with three homemade beautifully decorated, chocolate cupcakes. They were too beautiful to eat them by myself, so I took them home to share with my family.

Olive Oil and Other Delicacies

When people approach me and they taste some chestnuts, I ask them:
"Are you local?"

This time they answered:

"No, we are from the States. We come to Ottawa three, four times a year for vacation, and to buy olive oil here at 'La Bottega,' where they have a great variety to choose from.

Everybody Likes Them

Eugene is a disabled person. His body is racked with pain. We can't touch him or he will scream in pain. He came to see me in his wheelchair that he controls with his head. He calls from across George Street:

"Luziano! Luziano! Castagne!"

I prepare and wrap up 5-6 chestnuts for him and I place them in the front dash of his wheelchair. He thanks me and he goes into the Rideau Mall where someone will peel them and put them in his mouth.

He loves them! He doesn't miss one day when I am in the Market.

Food Tours

Occasionally, often I would say, there are food tours in the Market. The lady guides from "C'est bon!" come by before the tour to tell me that at a certain time they will be passing by with 3-4-7 people, or more. At the specified time they come around with the clients. They introduce me to them and then they allow me to talk about the "chestnut culture" and the different delicacies we can prepare with them.

Biscotti!

Every day, the first chestnuts I roast I give to the girls that work in the kitchen at "La Bottega." While they prepare the daily menu they also bake great, fresh *biscotti (biscuits)*. For every batch they make I am priviledged to have the end pieces of the different varieties they make. What a treat! Most of the time I take them home. I enjoy them soaked in wine. The rest I share with my family. They love them too!

Coupons

The manager of "Crazy Moose " came out of his store to tell me that he wanted to see me at some point during the day.

Time went by and I had the pleasant visit of a couple of friends that had just arrived from Italy to spend the Christmas holidays in Ottawa. I was at the end of my day. I asked if they knew the store. They vaguely answered that they did not know it. I invited them in for a visit and they were fascinated! The store manager gave them some 13% discount coupons that theyput to good use!

Eye Doctor

A man came around. He looked at the Christmas baskets in the window of "La Bottega."

"I need a bigger one. A more expensive one!"

"You can go inside and ask for it. If they don't have it they will make one for you." I told him.

"I need a big basket for my eye doctor and his staff! They saved my eyes. I won't be blind!" He rushed inside "La Bottega" to fulfill his wish!

A Young Boy and the Squirrels

A lady came around with her 5-6 year old boy.

"Roasted chestnuts!" she said.

"Yes Madam…Would you like to sample one?" I asked trying to establish eye contact with both of them.

The young boy was not interested.

While roasting the chestnuts I had an idea. I asked:

"Do you have squirrels where you live?"

"Yes, a lot!" the mother said looking at the child. He looked back at her nodding and smiling.

Contact was made!

"Would you like me to give you some chestnuts to feed the squirrels? You give them 2-3 a day, early in the morning and then you will see that they will come around scratching their belly for more, like this," I imitated a squirrel scratching his belly.

I gave his mother some chestnuts that, while I roast them, I discard because of their poor quality.

I repeated the gesture of imitating the squirrel while talking. The boy looked at me, smiling, appreciating it. He was converted. He was now interested to know more about the "chestnut culture."

"Here," I said, wrapping a hot chestnut in a paper towel and putting it in his hand, "cover it with the other hand."

The warmth of the hot chestnut was the last magic touch to happily introduce the young boy to the chestnut culture.

They left smiling, as the happy boy held the warm chestnut dearly in his hands.

I thought that for only a few seconds of that child happiness, humanity should stop all violence, all arms races!

The morning after, December 14, I read in the newspaper about the horrific shooting of innocent schoolchildren in Connecticut!

Canadian Chestnuts

On Dec. 21st, early in the morning, on my way to "La Bottega," I stopped by the "Byward Fruit Market" to say hello to my friend Isaac, the owner. When I entered the store I couldn't believe what I saw on the shelf on my right side: Canadian chestnuts!

"Canadian chestnuts?" I asked Isaac.

He replied with a smile:

"Yes, there they are! They arrived yesterday!"

What a coincidence! CTV had arranged an interview for the news at noon; they had asked me to talk about chestnuts. What a better occasion to talk about what I care the most: Canadian chestnuts!

I bought some chestnuts and I went to set up for my day of "chestnut roasting."

The host of the "News at Noon," Leanne Cusak, came by with her cameraman. I introduced the Canadian chestnuts and then talked about the Italian chestnuts followed by the singing part.

Leanne sang. I sang. We both sang:

Canadian Chestnut Groves. Photo: Greg MacG.

"Chestnuts roasting on an open fire….."

Passersby stopped watching us sing and wondering what was going on.

The following day a lady came around and, with a big smile, said:

"Oh! You are a famous man now! All the ladies will be jealous of you."

That day many peoples came to see me and to congratulate me for the interview and for the show.

The Canadian chestnuts are produced by the Erie Gardens on Lake Erie. They are great to roast; they have a texture and taste differently from the Italian chestnuts. Once roasted they peel very well. Personally I believe that they would be perfect for stuffing.

Ne Jamais refuser un geste de bonté!

Il faisait froid, humide, un jour de neige. Il y n'avait pas beaucoup de personnes dans le Marché, alors j'ai décidé de fermer. Pendant que j'attendais que le four se refroidisse, j'ai commencé à peler les marrons. Ils étaient faciles à peler.

Une dame se présente :

"Je suis heureuse de vous trouver ici! J'aimerais vous acheter des marrons".

"Je suis désolé Madame, je n'en ai plus…Avec cette température, il n'y a pas de clients qui achète des marrons."

"Ceux-ci, je veux ceux-ci. Je dois envoyer des marrons à Québec! J'ai promis. Des marrons grillés sur un feu en plein air!"

"Je suis désolé Madame, je ne peux vous les vendre, parce que je les ai déjà pelés, je ne peux vendre des marrons pelés."

"J'en ai besoin, je les veux."

"Bien, dans ce cas, je vous les donne gratuitement."

"Je vais vous les payer!".

'Je ne peux les vendre Madame, je vous les donne gratuitement, j'insiste", dis-je, pendant que je les emballais encore tout chauds et les lui remettais.

"Les voici." Je lui dis que j'ai appris à ne jamais refuser de faire un geste de bonté! "Alors, prenez-les, ils sont gratuits!"

"Merci", dit-elle, mais, comme elle partait, elle déposa un billet de 10$ dans le plat à pourboire.

"Merci", dit-elle en me souriant, "ne jamais refuser de faire un geste de bonté!"

Je ne pouvais rien dire. Et je ne pouvais refuser son geste de bonté. Le lendemain, elle est venue avec son mari. Ils étaient un couple d'apparence très distinguée.

"Nous sommes venus vous dire merci à nouveau. Les marrons que vous nous avez donnés sont maintenant à Québec. Ils feront la joie des membres de notre famille. Merci!"

Never Refuse an Act of Kindness!

It was a cold, damp, and snowy day. There were not many people in the Market, so I decided to close. While I was waiting for the *fornella* to cool down I started to peel the leftover chestnuts. They were peeling very easily.

A lady came by:

"I am so glad I found you! I want to buy some chestnuts."

"Sorry, madam. I don't have any…With this kind of weather there are no customers…."

"What about those. I want those. I have to send them to Quebec City! I promised them. Chestnuts roasted on an open fire!"

"Sorry, madam. I can't sell them to you because I peeled them. I can't sell peeled chestnuts."

"I need them. I want them."

"Well, in that case, I will give them to you for free."

"I will pay for them!"

"I can't sell them, madam. I will give them to you for free. I insist." I said, while bagging them still warm, and I gave them to her.

"There you are." I said to her that I learned to never refuse an act of kindness! "So, take them, they are free!"

"Thank you." She said, but, as she was walking away she threw a $10 bill in my "Tip can."

"Thank you." She said, smiling at me, "Never refuse an act of kindness!"

I could not say anything and I could not refuse her act of kindness either.

The next day she came by with her husband. They looked like a very distinguished couple.

"We came to say 'thank you' again. The chestnuts you gave me are now in Quebec City. They will make some of our family members very happy! Thank you."

From Vancouver!

A couple came walking toward me.

"Thank God you are here! I went to get him at the airport. He just flew in from Vancouver. As soon as he got in the car he asked me to take him here, to the Market, to see if you were here. He met you on November 11, Remembrance Day, and he wanted to come back to taste your 'freshly roasted chestnuts!.....'"

What can I say!......

Cold, Very Cold!

Some days it is very cold in Ottawa, in the Market in particular, considering that I operate on the North side were there is no sun at any time during the day.

A lot of people ask me:

"Aren't you cold?"

Actually I am not cold. I am well dressed with multiple layers of clothing that keep me warm. If I get cold, I just ask any of the workers at "La Bottega" for a cappuccino and a few minutes later there it is, delivered to me. It's a deliciously warm and smooth cappuccino.

I have my espresso in the morning made by Giovanni and in the afternoon I have my "delizioso cappuccino" made by my incomparable friend Zack.

Rachel

L'amour, comme la chance, ne peuvent se planifier…

Dimanche, une fin de semaine comme à l'habitude. Un jeune homme distingué, de bonnes manières, bien vêtu, est venu. Nous nous entendions très bien. Il savait ce qu'il voulait, un sac de marrons fraîchement grillés qu'il dégusterait tout de suite devant moi.

Elle s'est arrêtée à mes côtés, jeune et belle…

"Marrons?" Dit-elle. "Je n'ai jamais gouté."

Le jeune homme en a immédiatement et facilement ouvert un devant nous et le lui a présenté, encore inséré dans les deux parties de la coquille…

"Prenez-le", dit-il, "savourez-le, et faites un vœu."

Elle a adoré.

Le jeune homme est parti, elle est restée.

"Le connaissez-vous?"

"Il est mon client depuis quelques jours."

"Pensez-vous qu'il reviendra?"

"Je ne sais pas. Pourquoi?"

"Je suis de Montréal, je suis nouvellement arrivée ici à Ottawa, et ca ne me déplairait pas de rencontrer des gens comme lui."

"Bien…"

"Je vais vous donner mon numéro de téléphone. S'il vient par ici, svp lui demander de me téléphoner."

"C'est bien", dis-je.

Rachel écrivis son nom et son numéro de téléphone sur un reçu de "La Bottega" et elle me le donna.

"Au revoir". Elle s'en alla.

La semaine après, Rachel est venue me voir avec une dame. Elles se sont arrêtées. J'ai croisé le regard de Rachel.

"Bonjour Rachel, comment allez-vous?"

Elle n'a pas eu le temps de répondre. La dame qui l'accompagnait la regarda sévèrement et lui dit :"'Comment se fait-il qu'il connaît ton nom?

"Je t'expliquerai plus tard ... Maman!"

"Puis-avoir un sac de marrons? Ma mère n'en a jamais goûtés!"

Nous avons échangé marrons, argent et sourires... pendant que sa mère nous surveillait tout en se demandant ce qui se passait entre nous deux!...

Rachel

Love, like luck, can never be planned...

Sunday, my usual weekend. A distinguished, well mannered, well dressed, young man came by. We were very much connected. He knew what he wanted, a bag of freshly roasted chestnuts that he would start to eat right there in front of me.

She stopped at my side, young and beautiful...

"Chestnuts?" she said. "I never tasted one."

The young fellow immediately opened one very easily in front of us and presented it to her still in the two part shell...

"Take it." I said, "savour it, and make a wish."

She loved it.

The young man left, she stayed.

"Do you know him?"

"He has been my customer for the past few days..."

"Do you think he will be back?"

"I don't know. Why?"

"I am from Montreal. I am new in Ottawa, and I don't mind meeting people like him..."

"Well..."

"I will give you my phone number. If he comes around please ask him to call me."

"That's fine." I said.

Rachel wrote her name and her phone number on a "La Bottega" receipt and gave it to me.

"Au revoir." She left.

The following week Rachel came to see me with a lady. They

stopped. I made eye contact with Rachel.

"Hello, Rachel, how are you?"

She did not have time to answer. The lady that was with her looked seriously at her and said:

"How come he knows your name?"

"I will explain to you later…Maman!"

"Can I have a bag of chestnuts? My mother never tasted one!"

We exchanged chestnuts, money, and smiles….while her mother was watching us still wondering what was going on between the two of us!….

Street Drain

There is only one street drain along George Street. It is located in front of the "Pub Aube Dubliner." My professional responsibility as a "building operator" sometimes emerges for the comfort and safety of the people, expecially the disabled that visit and shop at the ByWard Market. So here I am keeping the street drain clean the best I can. I also try to make most people understand why they have to keep the drain clean during the week when I am not in the Market.

Snow Shovel

After the overnight snow storm, first thing this Friday morning, I went to check the street drain. It was covered with a lot of snow. I was very disappointed because I had no snow shovel to remove the snow and clear the drain.

A roofer company came to remove some scaffoldings in front of the "Aube Dubliner." After they removed the snow on top of the scaffolding they proceeded to cleaned the sidewalks very well. I was watching the whole process and the shovels that they were using. I wished I had one like that. I would have cleared the street drain! I approached the workers and I introduced myself. I knew and appreciated their company during my previous profession. I asked them to borrow the shovel for a few minutes so that I could clean the drain.They handed me one. I started to shovel the snow. The man that gave me the shovel went in the truck and took another one. In few minutes I had cleared the drain.

"I like this shovel." I said to the worker as I was giving it back to him.

"Keep it." He said.

"How much do I give you?"

"Two sandwiches at 'La Bottega!'"

"Done deal." I said.

Now I have a brand new shovel that I will use to keep the street drain clear of the snow!

The Elderly Lady

It was a miserable day, snow, wet snow, you name it.

I was serving some lady customer, one of them right in front of us. There she was, an old lady with one of those two-wheel grocery carts trying to step on the sidewalk in front of us. The sidewalk was full of compacted, slippery ice. She would never make it.

I went over and, very gently and very carefully, put my right arm under her left arm so as to give her some form of confidence and support.

She appreciated what I was doing and how I was doing it....

"Thank you." She said. "I didn't want to go out today...But I had no bread and milk at home!"

"I understand!" I said. And, for a moment I wondered if, one day, I would have the same problem.

Louise!

What a marvelous elderly person she is!

Elegant. She passes by almost every day when I am in the Market. She addressed me in Italian; she loves everything that is Italian. She is the one that gave me the book in which I found the chestnut roaster scene in Naples in which he serves two young ladies. It is a very precious image because it explains why and how to keep the chestnuts warm after they have been roasted.

Raymond, the "Tailor of Distinction"

I was talking with my friend Raymond, the "Tailor of distinction," and he said to me:

"My father told me that money does not make you rich. You are rich here and here ..", he said, pointing to his heart and his brain.

Every day a couple of elderly men pass by to keep Raymond company. They go to get a coffee and they always offer me one that I refuse. As soon as I have the first chestnuts ready I bring six to Raymond and his friends.

I don't have to say how much they appreciate them!

The Bread of the Poor

Once a person has savoured a chestnut, I suggest savouring it with some cheese because chestnuts were called the "bread of the poor or the bread from heaven!" Chestnut trees are big and they produce a lot of chestnuts. When they fall it looks like heaven is giving them to mankind.

I tried eating chestnuts with every kind cheese: Italian, French, hard, soft. I found the ideal combination to be chestnuts and a little morsel of the six year old Perron cheddar cheese that's made in Quebec and sold at "La Bottega." I usually chew chestnut and cheese together. I turn them into my mouth until they are well mixed. I savour the flavor and then I wash it down with a sip of red wine.

Simply sensational!

Most of the time, before I have even finished talking the person goes into "La Bottega" and comes out a few minutes later with the six years old Perron cheddar cheese.

"And the red wine?" I ask.

"I got some at home!"

Or,

"I will buy it on the way home!"

(P.S. Just late in the season of this year 2013, I visited the Perron cheese web site. Apparently it is the only cheddar cheese that is exported to England).

Superstition!

They stop to taste a chestnut. Wow!

"Is this the first time you taste a chestnut?"

"Yes."

"Make a wish."

"Why?"

"It is part of the Italian tradition of superstitions. Every time we taste something for the first time we make a wish, like when we sample 'il vino novello!' the new wine. On New Year's Day we eat lentil soup, a lot of lentils, a lot of money!"

"Does it work?"

"Well, last year, a lady came by, made a wish and a few

weeks later she came again."
"My wish came true. I am pregnant now!"
Most of the time people close their eyes and make a wish!
The power of the chestnut!

Like People!

As I am roasting chestnuts, a few people gather around me to watch. I explain that each chestnut roasts in a different way and once roasted they peel differently. Some are easy to peel, others are not that easy.
"They are like people," said a person.
"You are right! "I said. "We, are all different!"

Feet Warmers!

Sheila is a custom jeweler designer. She has her business in the Market building where the artisans are. She has been my customer ever since I started roasting chestnuts. She knows their nutritional value and every day when I am in the Market, I deliver her an order, one of the first orders of chestnuts I roast.
Today is very cold, bitterly cold! I deliver her the chestnuts and she asks me:
"Are you cold? Do you have feet warmers?"
"Feet warmers?"
"Yes, like these." She pulls out a package. "Here, try these and see if they work for you!"
I did what she told me and I followed the instructions on the package. They work!
"Thank you Sheila."
The day after it was still very cold! I went as usual to deliver the chestnuts to Sheila and she asked me:
"Do they keep your feet warm?"
I stopped and started to think and to feel if my feet were warm."Yes! My feet are very warm now! I don't know if it is because of the feet warmers or because of your generosity. I think it is your generosity!" I said looking into her eyes.
"Yes! It has to do with my generosity!" She said with her beautiful smile!

Paolo Copelli

Paolo Copelli was the ByWard Market manager when I came up with the idea of roasting chestnuts. I knew and I respect Paolo's family. I knew Paolo to be part of the "second generation of Italians in Ottawa." I knew that he had that very important function in the Market and I invited him to a presentation in front of "Pasticceria italiana" on Preston Street.

I asked Paolo if it was possible for me to roast chestnuts in the ByWard Market in front of "La Bottega." He went out of his way to make my dream come true.

Here I am now. Every morning the first chestnuts I roast go to Sheila and the other package to the members of the ByWard Market office staff. I must say that they appreciate them. Every time I deliver them, the staff, and the ambassadors take the chestnut package with a great "Thank you!" smile.

Recently

One of the Market ambassadors is my customer. He comes regularly to get them. The other day the weather was miserable and I could see him going around, in the snowstorm, with a shovel to keep strategic places in the Market clean. "What a job!" I said to myself.

Oh! There he is! He is passing by me.

"Here, take some chestnuts, they will do you good!"

"No, thanks, I have no time…"

"I insist you take them!" I said with a smile, and I added: "I am a citizen of Ottawa. I pay taxes. I pay your salary. So now you take a break!"

Knowing how hard he was working I kind of imposed my "citizen's authority" on the young man. He smiled at me, took the bag of chestnuts, put it in his coat pocket, and left with the shovel in his hand still smiling with great appreciation.

I hope he will have time to eat them before they get too cold.

Logistics

The fall of 2012 was not the easiest one. One or two days every weekend we had inclement weather so I had to stop roasting chestnuts and this made a lot of people unhappy! Some of my customers and friends suggested that I use a portable gazebo. I have one, but I don't want to put it in front of the historic facade of "La Bottega." I love the front of the store. I knew personally the last of the Saso family when he still had the store with all the memorabilia inside.

Back to reality.

So I had to close the roasting operation for the day.

The Two Gregs

I must say that to promote my love for chestnuts I need all the help I can get. Here I have to give credit and thanks to two of my friends Greg A., and Greg MacG. The two Gregs help me in two different ways.

To move the *fornella* I relay on Greg MacG. He has the truck and the ramps to facilitate the move from the Market to Villa Marconi where, every January, I roast chestnuts for the Italian senior residents. The day after Greg is there, at my house, ready to take the *fornella* back to "La Bottega."

I rely on Greg A. for other emergencies. On Sunday afternoons I could not leave the Market and disappoint the customers so I rely on Greg to deliver the freshly roasted chestnuts at Italian community gatherings.

Greg A. also helps me move the *fornella* with a van, for an Italian community event. I am not comfortable driving a van, so Greg does it for me!

Thanks to both Gregs!

The fornella

The *fornella*, where the wood-coal is burning, is a piece of "simple engineering." It is safe and easy to operate.It is very simple to adjust the fire, so it is easy to increase or decrease the heat

when I roast the chestnuts. The *fornella* has a swinging dish where I put the chestnuts between two fire proof blankets once they are roasted. I leave them there for a few minutes. The humidity will blend in with the starches and the sugars, the chestnuts will become softer, creamier and better tasting.

The *fornella* is mounted on a cart that has four wheels so it makes it easy to move.

Under the *fornella,* there is room for three plastic boxes. It is there that I keep all I need to exercise my profession as a chestnut roaster.

I must say that to be sure that the *fornella* operated safely, I had it inspected by the Licensing Office of the City of Ottawa that recommended and enforced some very useful and important changes.

Great New Ideas!

It was right before Christmas, when there are many office parties. A friend of mine came to see me and told me that he had the strange idea of taking some freshly roasted chestnuts to his office party.

"Will it be possible?" He asked.

"Well, we will make it possible." I said.

The day and time arrived. We were ready. I had a beautiful basket with all that was necessary to keep the chestnuts warm for a while.

My friend picked up the basket. We could smell the chestnuts while he was walking to the party.

The next day, when he brought back the empty basket, I asked him how it went.

"You should have seen the people! They literally jumped on the chestnuts, leaving all the other food there on the tables. They ate it only when there were no more chestnuts!"

What a success! What a surprise! I could not believe it myself!"

Give It to Charity!

She was young. She stopped to buy some chestnuts.

"A bag is $5 dollars."

She searched for the money and she could not find the right amount. She put her purse down and searched inside; she could not find the right amount! She was very, very disappointed!

"Don't worry. Here are the chestnuts. Put them in your coat pocket. Enjoy them. Put into the can whatever you have. What is missing give it to the charity of your choice."

She left smiling.

She came back shortly after. She gave me a $20.00 bill. I tried to give the right change back to her.

"No, no! Keep the $5.00 for the bag of chestnuts. What I gave you earlier is the tip." She said very determined.

What could I say... Never refuse an act of kindness!

Gambling!

....and the consequences!

He was there waiting, sipping his coffee. We talked. He used to be a carpenter, but now he is retired. We chatted while I got ready for the day. He told me about his life and how now he had problems with his legs.

I started the day. An Italian friend of mine passed by and saw the elderly man. They started to talk. They had known each other for a long time.

Once the elderly man left, my friend told me that the elderly man used to work for a contractor…that did not pay him what he was supposed to and, sometimes, the boss, did not pay him at all.

The boss, let's call him Joe, is now dead. Joe liked to gamble — that's where he lost all his money — even the money he was supposed to give to his workers.

My friend, told me that once he had taken the place of another player who had gone to the washroom and saw Joe lose $5.000.00…not once, but twice!

"Imagine! He lost $10.000.00! in a few minutes! And he did not pay his workers! But now he is dead!"

I could not answer. I was speechless! My friend left in the snowstorm…

"Arrivederci…"

The University of Ottawa

He was going around the ByWard Market with his tripod and his camera. He talked to a lady from "Canada Encounter" who was in Ottawa with a group of young students.

When he came close to me I asked him if he was with the group.

"No." He said, "I live here in Ottawa…"

We had a very interesting conversation. His name was Renault, he studied Sociology at the University of Ottawa, while his girlfriend was studying Psychology, and that he had a high regard for the quality of education he was receiving.

"It is the best University I know!" said Renault. "At he end of my studies I can get a Bachelor degree that has the value of two because I take English and French courses. At the end of my studies I can exercise my profession in the two languages so I have a double possibility of getting a job!"

It made sense to me. I would have liked to be Renault's age and start my life all over again!

* * *

I did not see him for a while; he came by; he stopped; we talked. I asked him where he was going to school and he told me that he was going to Ottawa U.

"What are you taking?"

"Linguistic Psychology."

"Linguistic Psychology?"

"Yes, Psychology is related to languages, and other disciplines..."

"Interesting. And how do you find the courses at U of O? Are you taking them in both languages?"

"Of course! By doing so I will have a better chance to be admitted for my Master at another University! I am now in my fourth year. I think I can be admitted to at least three other Universities!"

C'est bon! Tours

Today there were two "C'est Bon" tours. I felt very priviledged to talk to the people with the tour. They were very open to the "Chestnut experience" and I believe they enjoyed it.

Thank you all at "C'est bon!"

Bal de neige! Impressionnant!

Ils se sont arrêtés. Ils étaient de la région de Toronto; ils étaient à Ottawa pour le Bal de neige. Ils avaient leurs patins sur leur épaule.

"Êtes-vous allés patiner sur le Canal?"

"Oui..."

"Comment avez-vous aimé l'expérience?"

"Très impressionnant!...Nous avons adoré. Il y avait beaucoup de monde, c'était très beau! Et maintenant nous allons au Parc Jacques Cartier!"

"Passez un beau séjour à Ottawa..."

"Merci, jusqu'à maintenant nous nous amusons beaucoup!"

Winterlude! Impressive!

They stopped by. They were from the Toronto area. They were in Ottawa for "Winterlude."
They had their skates on their shoulder.
"Did you go skating on the Canal?"
"Yes..."
"How did you like it?"
"It was impressive!...We loved it. There were a lot of people. It was very beautiful. And now we will go to the Jacques Cartier Park!"
"Enjoy your stay in Ottawa...."
"Thank you, we did enjoy it very much so far!"

Bal de neige

Une famille s'est arrêtée, les parents, deux petites filles, et un autre bébé dans un harnais sur le dos du père. Ils s'arrêtent, curieux de voir ce que je faisais. Les deux petites filles étaient les plus intéressées, elles regardaient à travers la grille avec grande attention. Intelligence au travail!

J'ai commencé à expliquer la culture du marron et, tout en offrant deux marrons au papa pour qu'il les pèle et les donne 'aux dames!'

'Vous êtes un gentleman!, n'est-ce pas?

Nous nous sommes souris... Il a donnée les marrons aux dames, elles les ont beaucoup aimés. J'ai remarqué que la plus âgée des filles, elle avait 7-8 ans, ne portait pas ses gants, elle les avait dans sa poche. J'ai enveloppé deux marrons que je mis dans ses mains, son visage passa de la curiosité à un beau grand sourire. Elle sentait la chaleur des marrons dans ses mains, et elle souriait pendant qu'elle montrait ses mains à ses parents. Pendant ce temps, son père continuait à les nourrir de marrons qu'il pelait aussi vite qu'il le pouvait. Avant de partir, ils en achetèrent un sac.

En partant, l'autre fillette dit :

'Je me suis bien régalée!'

J'étais surpris et content pour elle, pour l'expérience positive

qu'elle venait de vivre et pour la façon dont elle exprimait ses sentiments. Je lui ai demandé son nom.
'Loryanne...'
'Et ta sœur?'
'Cassandra'
'Merci, vous ferez partie de ma chronique.'

Winterlude!

A family stopped by, the parents, two girls and a baby in his father's backpack. They stopped, curious about what I was doing. The two girls were the most interested. They were looking through the grill with great attention. Intelligence at work!

I started to explain the chestnut culture and, while doing so, I offered two chestnuts to the father to peel and serve them to the "ladies."

"You are a gentleman! Aren't you?"

We smiled at each other...He served the chestnuts to the ladies. They really enjoyed them. I noticed that the older girl, who was about seven or eight years old, had no gloves on as she had them in her pocket. I wrapped two warm chestnuts and I put them in her hands. Her face changed from curiosity to a great big smile. She felt the warm chestnuts in her hands, and she kept smiling as she showed her hands to her parents. Meanwhile her father continued feeding them chestnuts that he kept peeling as fast as he could. Before leaving they bought a bag.

While leaving, the older girl said:

"Je me suis bien regale!"

I was surprised and happy for her, for the positive experience she had just had and the way she expressed her feelings. I asked her name

"Loryanne..."

And your sister? "

"Cassandre."

"Thank you, you will be in my chronicle."

First Chestnuts of 2013

The first chestnuts I roasted in 2013 I gave to Zorica. She works in the kitchen at "La Bottega." Every time I offer her some chestnuts she thanks me with a big, sincere smile.

From the second batch I roast, I give six chestnuts to my friend Raymond "the tailor of distinction" so that he can enjoy them with his senior friends that come to see him every day.

The First Chestnuts I Roasted in Italia

"Il tempo in Italia si misura con le fasi politiche. I tempi sono ben precisi, determinati e determinanti. Ora abbiamo appena passato la fase del dibattito Bersani e Renzi. Ora aspettiamo un'altra fase!"

Il cellulare di Gianpaolo squilla. Gianpaolo risponde e si allontana per parlare tranquillo.

Ritorna dopo poco.

"Almeno qualcosa funziona! Era la mia banca in Italia che mi comunicava che la mia carta di credito era stata utilizzata a Ottawa, in Canada, per un prelievo. Li ho tranquillizzati."

Giovanni racconta che è appena tornato dall'Italia dove tutti fumano, anche in casa.

"Mia madre sgrida mio padre perché fuma in casa. Le sue sigarette puzzano!

Ma quelle dei figli, anche loro fumano in casa, quelle non puzzano. Protegge i figli, li vizia!

The First Chestnuts I Roasted in Italia

"Time in Italy is measured by the political cycles. The periods are precise, determined and determining. Now we are just over the debate between Bersani-Rienzi. Now we are waiting for a new cycle."

Gianpaolo's cell-phone rings. Gianpaolo answers and moves away to speak quietly.

He returns a little later.

"At least something works. It was my bank in Italy telling me that my credit card had been used in Ottawa, Canada, to take out money. I told them it was OK."

Giovanni tells us that he has just returned from Italy where everyone smokes, even in the house.

"My mother yells at my father because he smokes in the house. His cigarettes stink."

However whenever the children smoke in the house, their cigarettes do not stink. She protects the children. She spoils them!"

Wood Charcoal

He is my friend and he approached me while I was roasting chestnuts.

"What kind of charcoal are you using?"

"Wood charcoal. There is the bag."

"Because, you know, some coal has petroleum in it."

"I know."

"Can I see what coal you are using?"

"Here it is." I answered while lifting the grill part of the *fornella*. "You see?"

"Oh that's fine." He said after he had a good look at the coal that was burning in the *fornella*.

Buon anno (Happy New Year)

She went by me. She looked Asian.

"Buon anno," she said with a smile as she went by.

Dialogue, Debate, Fight!

Here I am involved once again in one of the many political and social discussions to pass the time.

I make the point that many politicians do not dialogue. They debate, or fight even over issues that are not important!

"Yes!" The man answered. "Just like it is happening now in many countries!"

Discovery

He was dressed all in white. He stopped for a second. I asked him his name. Alex looked like he was a chef in one of the restaurants in the Market. He was going to "La Bottega" to buy some special products. I offered him some chestnuts to take to his colleagues. He accepted. While roasting them I explained to him their benefits and how they should be prepared. I introduced him to the side dish "Chestnuts and Brussel sprouts."

What a discovery this was for Alex! He left very happy!

The Boot Lady

I like her very much. She is a frail, elderly lady. She passes by every day, weather permitting. I give her four chestnuts in a paper bag, well wrapped in a napkin. Then she gives me a plastic bag that she puts into another one. When she leaves she says:

"I will give them to my son. I will pay you on my way back."

She never did pay me. I don't mind.

Today she came by. The same routine.

She told me that she was going to get some work done on her feet. When she came back she told me that she felt strange. Someone may have exchanged her boots!

What could I say?

The next day she passed by. The same chestnuts routine. I asked her about the boots.

"Oh! They are mine. My feet felt differently because they worked them in! They are mine!"

What can I say?

From Australia with Love

She is a good customer of "La Bottega." Today, once her shopping was done, she went by me. We nodded "Hello!"

Then she came back.

"Your chestnuts are very good!" She said. "I bought two bags for Christmas and I offered some to my friends from London (ON). They loved them! They were from Australia. They were visiting Canada. They loved your chestnuts. They found them better than the Australian ones!"

"Thank you, madame," I said, and I thought:

"From Australia with love!"

She surrendered to her temptation!

"Can I have a bag, please?"

I served her. While serving her I asked her for her name. I wanted to quote her in my chronicles. She declined. She did not want to have her name mentioned.

I understand. Once, and if published, I will give her a copy.

Mother and Daughter

They came by, the middle aged, very distinguished daughter, with her mother.

I was getting ready for the day.

"Can you come back in ten, fifteen minutes?"

"Yes, we will."

A few minutes later the daughter came by. She took two bags and went in a parked car in front of me.

I had to deliver some chestnuts. I had to pass by the parked car. And there they were, munching away, in the car. I looked at the daughter and I made a thumbs up sign.

"Yes." She said, lowering the window, "They are excellent, my mother loves them too!".

Her mother smiled at me.

Mother, Son and Modern Society

The mother was kind of pointing her son into one of the stores near where I was standing. She came back a few minutes later.
"Roasted chestnuts?"
"Yes, madame, freshly roasted chestnuts!"
"We have them everywhere in our country in South America, and we love them!"
So we started to talk.
"I took my son for an interview and I hope they will hire him!" She said to me. "He spends most of the time of the day with his friends playing games on the computer! He has to get a life! At his age he should be doing something worthwhile!"
I couldn't agree more. This mother loves her son so much and yet her son is wasting his life playing computer games!
We, MY generation, gave everything we had to make a life worth living, all the commodities, food, equipment to cook, to learn, to live, and learn to live with dignity! And what is this young person doing?
Wasting his life using the valuable resources we provide him with!

Two Men and a Chestnut

He stopped by. He had a lot of questions that required answers. He was well- dressed, polite. We chatted. I think I stimulated his interest in the "chestnut culture."
Another man came by. He bought a bag of chestnuts. I got him involved in the "Educational dialogue" I was having with the other man.
After a while I noticed that one big chestnut I was roasting was just perfect, ready to be savoured.
I picked it up and I handed it to the man that had just bought the bag, and said to him:
"There are two of them in this one. Peel it, you take this one, the bigger one, and give the other one to this gentleman."
He followed my instructions. There they were, in front of me, savouring freshly roasted chestnuts. They looked ecstatic. They loved them!

When they "came back to reality" I suggested to them to continue savouring the chestnuts with some six years old Perron cheddar cheese, sold at "La Bottega," followed by a sip of red wine to wash their mouth.

The first man said:

"I must get some money from my wife. I will be back."

He was back with his wife a few minutes later, and he started lecturing her on the nutritional and other values of the chestnuts and how to enjoy them.

What an ambassador he was!

Coupons!

Here they were on the sidewalk, looking at me, puzzled.

"What time does the store open?"

They asked me pointing to the "Crazy Moose" store.

"Any moment." I said.

"We have to be back at the hotel soon, we have no time!"

With great indifference I started to "entertain" them, a man and three young boys.

"Are you local?" I asked.

"No. We are from Frankfurt, Germany."

"Been there, seen that. I am from Italy between Venice and Austria. I used to speak German when I was young. I loved it."

The conversation went on but I could feel that the man was nervous. He had to go back to the hotel…and I was running out of ways to entertain them.

I offered them a "Crazy Moose" coupon.

"With this coupon you can get 13% discount on all merchandise in the store, even the ones that are on special!"

Done.

I got their attention.

Once I realized that I had their attention, I noticed that Bill, the manager of "Crazy Moose," was walking toward us.

"There is Bill." I said to the man.

"Who?"

"Bill, the manager, who will open the store for you."

Naturally the men did not recognized Bill. He was also dressed for the snowstorm that was about to hit Ottawa.

Bill opened the store and, a few minutes later, they were inside. Somehow, the man did not have to rush back to the hotel any more.

Later on in the day, Bill told me how much he appreciated what I had done to "entertain" those very valuable customers! And yes. They used the coupon I gave them!

To Cultivate (Growing Chestnut Trees)

For me chestnut roasting is a good excuse to promote, what I call, "The chestnut culture," and I take every opportunity to do so!

But to make the campaign to promote the chestnut culture more effectively, I planted some chestnuts that are now trees!

I did plant some chestnut trees that I have grown from Italian chestnuts over the years; they are now trees, some of them a few feet high.

"Would I ever eat chesnuts from them?" I often ask myself.

In 2012 I planted several trees, 6 or 7 of them on the shore of the Rideau River. In the spring of 2013 I will go and see if they are growing as well as the ones I have planted in my back yard in 2011.

I keep a complete list of all the chesnut trees I plant in friends' places and in other places. Grimo Nursery sent me two "grown in Canada" trees that are a cross breed with the chinese chestnuts.

I Wish....

She passes by.
"Chestnuts?" "Would you like to try one?" I offer her one.
She peels it, she savours it, she enjoys it!
"Make a wish. It is part of the Italian tradition, superstition..."
I also tell her that a bag wil cost $5.00.
"I'll take a bag."
I prepare her a bag. I go in the front of the *fornella*. I put the bag in her left coat pocket. She counts the money and puts it in the can.
"Did you make a wish?" I asked her.
"My husband took my daughter. I wish he will bring her back to me."
We looked at each other.
We found ourselves in each other's arms, in tears.
"God bless you!" I said, parting from her.
I could not hold my emotions.
I glanced at her.
She had tears running down her face.
I turned my back to her.
I was in tears myself.
I was emotionally overwhelmed, and I still am now, while I recall this chronicle to share with you.
I really hope her wish will come true!

Vermont!

A young couple approached me.
"Chestnuts?" I offered them one. They loved it!
"I will take a bag." She said.
"It is $5,00."
" Do you take credit cards, interact..."
"No. I am sorry. Mine is a very simple operation. Please take the bag, don't worry, if you happen to pass by with the money it is OK, if not, consider it a gift from me. Are you local? Are you from this region?"

"No. We are from Vermont, USA"

"Been there, seen that, and loved it!"

I gave them another chestnut each, and I told them where they could find an ATM machine. But I said:

"Don't worry! Enjoy your visit to Ottawa!"

Not too long after, I was busy with other customers, a lady passed by with a $5.00 bill in her hand. She handed it to me. I did not recognized her. We made eye contact. I then recognized her. She was the one from Vermont, and she had come back to pay me.

Magog

"Des marrons? Je n'en ai jamais goûté!"

"SVP, goûtez-en quelques uns." J'en ai offert quelques uns à ce monsieur. Je lui ai montré comment les peler et lui ai dit de les offrir à sa famille, une dame et deux garçons.

Nous avons fraternisé.

Ils étaient de Magog. Je leur ai dit que j'étais allé là-bas plusieurs fois et que j'avais aimé voir tous ces gens prenant d'assaut la rue principale pendant l'été, en s'amusant.

"Tout comme en Italie! Le centre ville est redonné aux gens! J'aime beaucoup!"

"Nous faisons encore cela," a dit la dame, "et nous aimons beaucoup cela!"

Ils achetèrent un sac de marrons, ils sont allés sur le Canal et ils sont revenus en acheter encore d'autres! Ils les ont adorés, m'ont-ils dit!

Magog

"Chestnuts? I have never tried them!"

"Please, have a sample." I offered a couple of samples to the gentleman. I told him how to peel them and to offer them to his family, a lady and two boys.

We conversed.They were from Magog. I told them that I went there several times and that I loved to see all the people in the main street during the summer enjoying themselves.

"Just like in Italy. The center of the city is given back to the people. I love it."

"We are still doing it." The lady said, "and we enjoy it very much!"

They bought an order of chestnuts, they went on the Canal and then came back for more chestnuts! They loved them, they told me.

Un buon caffè all'italiana!

Passa, tutto ben imbaccuccato. Fa freddo! Molto freddo!

In un ottimo italiano mi chiede:

"È italiano Lei? Mi può dire dove posso bere un buon espresso all'italiana...Ma all'italiana!" Insiste.

"Venga, è al posto giusto. Venga, venga, glielo offro io con gran piacere!"

Così dicendo gli faccio da guida per l'entrata di servizio de "La Bottega." Entrando gli chiedo

"È di Ottawa?"

"No. Io sono di Mogadiscio. Ho due sorelle che abitano qua a Ottawa. Sono qua in visita."

Una volta entrati ne "La Bottega" chiedo a Zach di fargli un buon caffè e di metterlo sul mio conto.

Poco dopo il signore esce ringraziandomi per l'ottimo espresso che ha avuto modo di gustare.

"È bene sapere che qui posso bere dell'ottimo caffè. Grazie."

A Good Italian Espresso!

He passed by, well dressed for the cold day, for the very cold day!

In very good Italian he asked me:

"You are Italian? Can you tell me where I can get a good espresso...But, Italian espresso!" He insisted.

"Come with me, you are at the right place. Come, come, I will offer it to you, it will be my pleasure!"

While doing so I guided him to "La Bottega" through the service entrance. While entering I asked him if he was "local" from Ottawa.

"No. I am from Mogadishu. I have two sisters here in Ottawa and I am visiting them."

Once inside "La Bottega" I asked Zack to make him an espresso and put it on my account.

Shortly after the gentleman came out to thank me for the excellent espresso that he had tasted and enjoyed.

"It is nice to know that here I can have a great espresso. Thank you."

Castagnaccio!

Saturday and Sunday February 16 and 17, I prepared some *castagnaccio* to give away to clients and customers. They appreciated it very much and, even if the weather was very cold, they stayed with me to enjoy this delicacy.

Castagnaccio (Tuscany)

This Tuscan recipe was presented from "La Bottega" in the ByWard Market by Luciano Pradal to the people of Ottawa on October 22nd 2011 during the ByWard Market Oktoberfest.

Ingredients:

Chestnuts flour	*500g*
Water	*500 to 800ml*
Sultan raisins	*a hand full*
(Soaked in warm water or in white wine)	
Pine nuts	*100 or 50 g*
Walnut pieces	*100 or 50g*
Olive oil	*6-7 table spoons*
Fresh rosemary leaves	

This recipe calls for salt and sugar but we did not add it. You can add salt, maple syrup, small pieces of nuts, pistachio or any other of your favourite nuts.

Fresh rosemary leaves and a few little branches on top for decoration and flavor.

Procedure:

Soak the sultan raisins in warm water or in white wine for half an hour.

Sift the chestnuts flour into a bowl, add the water until you obtain a liquid mixture.

Add the raisins previously strained, the pine nuts, pieces of walnuts, the rosemary leaves and the olive oil; make sure you keep some of all of the above for the final decoration.

*Mix well until you obtain a smooth mixture; pour it, one centimeter thick.
In a previously well- oiled pan, decorate the surface with the pine nuts, the
raisin, the walnut pieces and little branches or leaves of rosemary; sprinkle some
olive oil on top.*
Put it in a previously preheated oven at 200C for half an hour or until the
castagnaccio *starts to get dry and form some cracks.*

A legend, dating back to 1449, says that the man that eats
castagnaccio offered to him by a lady, will fall in love with her and
he will marry her!

Castagnaccio is baked, not fried, no animal fat, no gluten, no
yeast. The scent and flavor of the rosemary will remind one of
summer and of sunny days.

Other than all the nutritional value of the chestnuts, the glu-
cide present in the chestnuts is released slowly in the human
body. They give slow and steady energy. This is ideal to overcome fatigue for people that exercise. *Castagnaccio* is good to
equilibrate the nervous system, for anemia, and osteoporosis.

They stayed with me while I explained why I had to stop
roasting chestnuts. The chestnut season was at an end. The quality of the chestnuts was deteriorating and I only wanted to provide the best I could, but it was impossible, so I had to say good
bye!

Winterlude 2013!

I would call it a great success!

I consider Ottawa a city "second to none!" And, during Winterlude 2013, we had proof! Ottawa was invaded by a lot of visitors from all over the world and a lot from…Toronto! I said a lot
from TO!

….And the Senators, right this weekend, lost the hockey
game to Toronto 3-0!

Imagine the Torontonians visiting Ottawa! What a great opportunity they had to proudly wear the Maple Leaf jersey…in
Ottawa!

Well, those things happen!

Sandro Zoppi, Family and Friends

For Sandro Zoppi, family and friends, for several years now, Ottawa has became the place to spend the long weekend in February. It started a few years ago when they visited the city, and I had the priviledge to serve as a guide for them, to discover Ottawa.

Sandro owns "Go By Bus," a bus touring company. He organizes several bus tours every year to visit Ottawa and the Region. I have the priviledge to be a guide for those tours.

Always, as soon they arrive in Ottawa, the first stop is at "La Bottega" for an espresso...and some freshly roasted chestnuts!

This weekend was the same. They arrived, they had some chestnuts and then, after some photos around *la fornella*, they went inside for an espresso.

They all had a lot of fun at Park Jacques Cartier, skating on the canal and doing numerous other activities. On Sunday afternoon they came by for more chestnuts. I was about to close because the quality of the chestnuts was not the best. I apologized to Sandro for not having enough chestnuts for all his family and friends.

"Don't worry, Luciano, we are here not only for the chestnuts but also for the beautiful experience and the good time we are having during this weekend here in Ottawa. Thank you from all of us!" said Sandro.

Having a bad dream!

On February 17 I stopped roasting chestnuts earlier. It was my last day of the season. Due to the very poor quality of the chestnuts, I decided to close earlier.

Once all was put away I went into "La Bottega" to thank Rocco Nicastro for all the cooperation and support the Nicastro family had given me for the 2012-2013 chestnut season.

"Why are you closing? Have you finished for the season? How come?"

Rocco could not believed that it was the end of the season. I tried to explain to him the circumstances and the reasons for my decision...

"I think I am having a bad dream!" Said Rocco while we were shaking hands.

"Arrivederci a presto!"

Emilio!

Emilio lavora a "La Bottega." Emilio ha una maniera tutta particolare, unica e simpatica, di lavorare, di vivere, di interagire con la gente e di sorprendere tutti con le sue battute.

Un giorno esce per fumare una sigaretta. Davanti a me è stazionata una Bugatti.

"Ti piacerebbe avere una Bugatti?" Chiedo ad Emilio.

"Io ho già le tasche.... bucate...(Bucate-Bugatti?).."

Questa mattina arrivo presto a "La Bottega" e devo passare per l'entrata di servizio nel retro del negozio. Entrando trovo Emilo che è già al lavoro.

"Ciao, Emilio. Sono sorpreso di vederti così presto e già al lavoro!.."

"Anch'io sono sorpreso di me stesso!...."

Emilio

Emilio works at "La Bottega." Emilio has a particular, unique and very happy way to work, to live, to interact with people and to surprise everyone with his sense of humor.

One day he comes out for a cigarette. In front of me is parked a Bugatti.

" Emilio, would you like to own a Bugatti?" I asked him.
"I own already a Bu...gat...ti." He pointed to his pant's pockets...Holes in his pockets.

This morning I arrived early at La Bottega. I entered by the back service door and saw Emilio already hard at work.

"Ciao, Emilio. I am surprised to see you so early and already at work!"

" Me too! I am surprised as well! "

Parking!

Every Friday and Saturday I park at the City Parking garage on Clarence Street, in the Market. Today, Saturday February 9, I did the same. My movements are well calculated by the weekly routine. Not one movement that is not necessary. They are all calculated.

I went to do my daily work.

Late in the afternoon, Beatrice, my granddaughter, called me: "Can you please pick me up on your way home?"

She has her first job at her age. She sells "Beaver Tails" on the canal during Winterlude. She loves the experience. She loves beaver tails.

Anyway I told her that I would pick her up in 15-20 minutes.

I walked to the City Parking garage on Clearance. I took my parking ticket out of my plastic folder. I fed it into the machine. It displayed that I had to pay $11.00.

I put in one $10.00 bill, it took it, remaining amount $1.00. I put in $1.00, still the same sign $1.00. I put in another dollar and it asked for another dollar! Another dollar! Another dollar! Another dollar!

Anyway, to make a long, very long story short, I had to cancel a few transactions and start all over again several times. Each time I lost $10.00.

I was upset, not only for the money I lost, but also because Beatrice was waiting for me after her work.

This was the first time I had this kind of bad experience with the parking machine. I just want to share it with you because you too may have had a similar experience!

Two Girls from Alberta!

Ottawa! Capital of the world!

Two young girls approached me while I was roasting chestnuts.

"Chestnuts?"

You know what happens. I offer one, they love it, we chat, I offer them more.

They loved their "chestnut experience" on the street of Ottawa. They were from Alberta. They loved Ottawa during Winterlude! They were very well at ease; we had a good conversation.

They wanted to put some coins in the can. I said:

"Please, you don't owe me anything. I offered them to you with great pleasure! Please…."

One started to put some coins into the can, the other did the same. I kept telling them that it was not necessary. But no. They had to "reward me" for the nice experience they had, here, in Ottawa, in the ByWard Market…So they told me while they were leaving, smiling!

Chronical Part of a Dialogue

A moment of quiet. No customers.Here I am, thinking about the chronicles that I will write, the notes I take, the social interaction that is generated, and that I love so much! I take out pen and paper and I write: "I think that those chronicles are part of a dialogue, a positive dialogue. But, is it always positive? I want those chronicles to be a positive dialogue."

Spicy!

As you may have already understood, while I roast chestnuts, I meet all kinds of people, and I love it!

One day two gentlemen approached me.

"Chestnuts?"

There we go! At a certain moment I told one of them:

"You have a peculiar accent.."

"Peculiar? I am from the UK!"

"Uhm...I understand..."

They were very nice gentleman. I felt that they were enjoying the experience, so I asked one of them very slowly, with great and effective eye contact:

"Can you, please, tell me why English people named the chestnuts after ... the two ... most popular ... parts of the ... human ... body ... Chest ... nuts... "and I accompanied what I said with gestures.

The gentleman said:

"I don't know."

And then with great and effective eye contact he directed my sight to a big building on my right. I looked at it and then I looked back at him.

"What?"

"You don't see the sign? What does it say?"

"CONDOMS!" I said...He did not say a word. They left!

Bolts, Nuts!

Renato is a great friend of mine. He is from Venice. He is also a great welder. Actually everything he does he does it well, very well! (Renato, if you read this, it is not a compliment!)

Anyway, a handle of the door of my *fornella* broke, so I took

the part and I asked Renato to weld me a piece of steel, so that the *fornella* would be operational again.

The next day Renato gave me back the door with the handle fixed. On the handle he welded two bolt "nuts" side by side! He gave it to me saying:

"Handle them carefully! Because those two "NUTS" are mine! So handle them carefully!"

What could I say?

Soaked Chestnuts

On the right side of the *fornella* I have a little table. On it I have a photo of a scene in Italy where the *castagnaro* serves two ladies. One of them has an apron where the *castagnaro* puts in the freshly roasted chestnuts so they "stew" for a few minutes before the are eaten. With it I have information about the chestnut's nutritional value in English and French. I also have a bag of chestnut flour, two cans of *purée de marrons*, a bag of dry chestnuts and a jar of chestnuts soaked in rum!

This jar is very appealing to many customers and they ask me how to do them.

It is very simple.

You roast the chestnuts, peel them, put them in a pot with whatever liqueur you like: rum, Grand Marnier, Cointreau, grappa, wine, etc., bring them to boil for a few minutes, remove form the heat, let it cool. Take the chestnuts and place them into a glass jar, take the liqueur that is in the pot and filter it with a cotton swab or a filter coffee. Once filtered, put it into the jar with the chestnuts, fill the jar with any other liqueur.

Leave the chestnuts in the liqueur for a few days so that the starches of the chestnuts absorb the alcohol and by doing so they will dissolve the sugars that are in the chestnuts.

After a few days you will have the chestnuts tasting the liqueur in a sweet syrup. Now you take an ice-cream bowl, put some ice cream in it, put a chestnut on top and some syrup around it. Bon appétit!

You can also serve the chestnuts on a cold anddamp afternoon when the body metabolism is down. Well, take one or two

chestnuts soaked in liqueur, the scent of the alcohol will activate
your metabolism and you will start to digest the nutrients of the
chestnuts. And that will help you overcome fatigue.
Once I was describing all those benefits to a group of ladies.
One of them asked me if I was a doctor. I told her:
"No, I am not a doctor, but this is what they were doing back
then when there was not central heating in the homes. People
learned how to keep warm and healthy quickly and efficiently."

Belle, buone e tutte sane!

Arriva, mi sembrava un po' teso.
"Sono venuto a prendere del parmigiano, me lo stanno grat-
tuggiando. La mia macchina è mal parcheggiata. Tienila d'occhio
per favore."
"Qual'è?"
"Quella con la finestra dietro aperta."
"Non ho visto gli agenti del parcheggio oggi. Forse oggi sono
tolleranti."
L'ho rassicurato.
"Posso offriti una castagna? Sono pronte e stufate a per-
fezione."
"Grazie," dice prendendone un paio, "mia moglie ne ha
comperate la settimana scorsa nei negozi, erano tutte marce! Ne
ha comperato un sacchetto da te ed erano belle, buone e tutte
sane!"
"Faccio del mio meglio per offrire il miglior prodotto possibile ai miei clienti. Visto che ti intendi di castagne, da che parte
dell'Italia vieni?"
"Sono parmense. Abbiamo molti castagneti dalle nostre
parti. Noi affumichiamo le castagne con la legna del castagno.
Mettiamo le castagne in speciali graticole e sotto facciamo fuoco
con la legna del castagno. Il fumo sterilizza le castagne che, così
facendo, si conservano più a lungo!"

Beautiful, Tasty, and no Rotten Ones!

He arrived, he look tense:
"I came to get some Parmesan cheese. They are grating it. My car is not properly parked. Can you keep an eye on it, please?"
"Which one is it?"
"The one with the back window open."
"I did not see any PCO. Maybe they are tolerant today." I reassured him
"Can I offer you a chestnut? They are ready and well stewed."
"Thank you," he said taking a couple. "My wife bought some last week in a grocery store but they were all rotten. I bought a bag from you and they were beautiful. They tasted fine, and not a single one was rotten."
"Well," I said, "I do the best I can to provide the best product possible to my customers. It looks like you are very knowledgeable about chestnuts. Where do you come from in Italy?"
"I am from Parma. We have a lot of chestnut groves where I come from. We smoke the chestnuts with chestnut's wood. The smoke sterilizes the chestnuts and by doing so they last longer!"

Charming

She is a charming elderly lady. I treat her every time she comes by. I give her a few chestnuts for herself and for her son. She promises me that she will pay me....Tomorrow.
Today she came by. I started to prepare some chestnuts.
"I don't have the bag with me."
"Don't worry. I will pack them well for you."
"How are you doing with this cold weather? I haven't been out of the house for ten days! I will go back in as soon I have done some shopping."
Not too long after she passed by on her way back. She waved at me.
"Hurry, go home fast, it is getting colder!" I said to her. Her hands and her face were red because of the cold weather.

"Un échantillon"

Tous les jours, je pèle des marrons fraichement grillés, je les garde à portée de main pour montrer à un client éventuel, à quoi ressemble un marron.

Aujourd'hui, un client régulier est venu avec une dame. Ils avaient leurs patins sur l'épaule,

"Bonjour, êtes-vous allés patiner sur le Canal?"

"Oui! Et nous avons beaucoup aimé. Il y avait beaucoup de monde à patins, ce qui est encore plus plaisant! Puis-je avoir mes deux sacs de marrons, comme a l'habitude, svp?"

Pendant que je préparais ses deux sacs, il prit un 'échantillon de marrons' et a essayé de le mettre dans sa bouche.

"Non", j'ai dit, "ne mange pas celui-ci! C'est un échantillon. Il est froid. Voici, prends-en et offres-en à la dame."

Il en pris quelques uns, chauds entre du réchaud du fourneau, les pela et les donna à sa dame.

"Goutes-y, tu les adoreras!"

Elle les aima tellement qu'elle en acheta un sac.

"D'où venez-vous?" Lui demandai-je.

"Du Québec."

"D'où exactement au Québec?"

"Thetford Mines."

"Thetford Mines? Mon épouse vient de St-Pierre de Broughton, c'est tout près!"

"Que le monde est petit", dit-elle.

The Sample!

Every day I peel a freshly roasted chestnut and I keep it handy to show a "prospective" customer what a chestnut looks like.

Today a regular customer came by with a lady. They had their skates on their shoulders.

"Good morning. Did you go skating on the canal?"

"Yes! And we enjoyed it very much. There were a lot of people skating, which makes it for more fun! Can I have my usual two bags, please?"

While I was preparing the two bags he took the "sample

chestnut" and tried to put into his mouth.
"No!" I said. "Don't eat that one! That's a sample. It is cold.
Here, serve yourself and also serve the lady."
He took a few, warm chestnuts from between the blankets
on the *fornella,* peeled one and gave it to his friend.
"Taste it, you will love them!"
She got hooked, she bought a bag.
"Where are you from?" I asked her.
"From Quebec."
"Where in Quebec?"
"Thetford Mines."
"Thetford Mines? My wife comes from S.Pierre de
Broughton, that's not too far!"
"It is a small world," she said.

Diaspora!

He was outside "La Bottega," waiting.
He was waiting.
I approached him:
" Hello, where are you from?"
"Upper State, New York, USA."
"I see." I tried to engage him.
"In 1987 we went cycle-camping Ottawa- Washington, 1000
kms...."
He was polite but not impressed the way I would have liked.
Maybe he was thinking how long he had still to wait!
"My grandmother, from my mother side, was born in New
York in 1890....." I said.
"My grandfather came from Germany in 1890." He replied.
He kept waiting. Then he came close to me.
"My ancestors came from France in 1560!" He told me be-
fore he joined his wife and left.
What a diaspora! Well... he surprised me!

Mario! Mario! Che tortura!

Esce per prendere una boccata d'aria fresca, forse un po' troppo fresca! Fredda! Gelata!

"A 'La Bottega' hanno un nuovo prosciutto di Parma, si chiama *Addobbo* è delizioso, speciale, te ne porterò un paio di fettine..."

Mi dice Mario, prima di affrettarsi a rientrare a "La Bottega" dove si occupa degli affettati.

Aspetto le fettine di prosciutto che Mario mi ha promesso.

Aspetto, con l'acquolina in bocca, le fettine di prosciutto che Mario mi ha promesso.

Aspetto!

Aspetto!

Avvicino Mauro, uno dei colleghi di Mario:

"Di' a Mario che Luciano sta soffrendo. Aspetta sempre le fettine di prosciutto *Addobbo* che gli ha promesso!"

Ci sorridiamo, Mauro ha capito che stavo scherzando.

Aspetto.

Aspetto ancora.

Incrocio Mario:

"Mario, mi stai torturando. Sto ancora aspettando le fettine di prosciutto che mi hai promesso." Gli dico in un tono scherzosamente serio."

Dopo quache minuto Mario viene fuori con un sacchetto di carta per panini. Entriamo, fuori fa troppo freddo.

"Vedi, ti ho messo una fetta di focaccia fresca, appena sfornata, con dentro una fettina di provolone dolce ed un paio di fettine di prosciutto *Addobbo*." Mi dice porgendomi la delizia.

Apro la focaccia, prendo una fettina di prosciutto, la guardo, l'annuso, la gusto piano piano cercando di coglierne i sapori e, perché no, anche qualche difetto. L'assaggio. Il prosciutto si scioglie in bocca con un sapore delicato ed uniforme non troppo secco né troppo grasso. Lo gusto nei minimi dettagli, in maniera approfondita, cerco di percepire il sale ed altre spezie, impossibile! Il gusto è uniforme, perfetto! Mentre assaporo pienamente la mia esperienza gastronomica Mario mi confida:

"Luciano, ho dovuto aspettare che il prosciutto si prestasse al miglior taglio, non troppo all'inizio del prosciutto e non troppo alla fine ..."

Ascolto, non rispondo, assaporo.
Mario mi guarda con viva curiosità.
"...Allora?" Mi chiede.
"È un prosciutto speciale. È valsa la pena d'avere l'acquolina in bocca per tutto questo tempo. Grazie Mario!"
Qualche giorno dopo, mia moglie va a trovare sua sorella in campagna e, come in ogni occasione, mando del prosciutto e dei grissini ad Angelo, mio cognato che è bolognese ed è un esperto per quanto riguarda il prosciutto. Questa volta gli mando il prosciutto *Addobbo*.
Il giorno dopo Angelo mi telefona per dirmi quanto gli è piaciuto il prosciutto *Addobbo*. Gli è piaciuto moltissimo! La maniera in cui era stato affettato, la quantità del grasso, il delicato profumo di mandorla della carne e la maniera che si scioglieva in bocca. Penso che questa volta Mario abbia fatto felice qualcuno!

Mario! Mario! What a Torture!

He comes out for a few minutes to get some fresh air. Maybe the air is too cool! Cold! Freezing! He goes back inside but he has time to tell me that at "La Bottega" they now have a new prosciutto from Parma called *Addobbo*. It is delicious, special!
"I will bring you one or two slices...." Mario tells me before he re-enters "La Bottega" in a hurry, where he looks after the cold cuts counter. I wait for the slices of prosciutto that Mario promised me!
I wait, with my mouth watering, for the slices of prosciutto that Mario promised me!
I wait!
I wait!
I approach Mauro, Mario's colleague:
"Tell Mario that Luciano is suffering. He is waiting for the slices of the prosciutto *Addobbo* that you promised him!"
We smile at each other as Mauro understands that I am joking.
I wait.
I wait
I meet Mario:
"Mario you are torturing me! I have been waiting for the

slices of prosciutto that you promised me." I told him in a jokingly but serious way!

After a few minutes Mario surprises me. He comes out and he gives me a sandwich bag. We enter the hallway since outside is too cold.

"You see, I got some fresh focaccia, it has just come out of the oven! Inside I put a slice of sweet provolone and two slices of prosciutto *Addobbo*." Mario says while handing me the delicacy.

I open the focaccia and take out a slice of prosciutto. I look at it, I smell it, I put it in my mouth and I taste it slowly, very slowly trying to capture the flavors and, perhaps, even some flaws if there are any.

I taste it, I savour it. The prosciutto is melting in my mouth with a delicate and uniform flavour, not too dry not too fat. I taste it very slowly, in every detail. I try to taste the salt and other spices. Impossible! The taste is uniform, perfect!

As I am fully enjoying my gastronomical experience, Mario says:

"Luciano, I had to wait until the prosciutto was ready for the best cut, not at the beginning, not at the end of the prosciutto....."

I am listening to "the voice of experience." I don't answer. I am savouring.

Mario looks at me curiously.

"....So?" He asks me.

"Fantastic! Excellent! You were right to tell me that it is a very special prosciutto! It was worth it to keep my mouth watering all this time. Thank you Mario!"

A few days later my wife had to see her sister at the farm, Every time I send some prosciutto and grissini to Angelo, my brother in law. He is from Bologna and he is a "prosciutto connoisseur." This time I sent him this new "*Addobbo*" prosciutto.

The next day Angelo phoned me to tell me how much he enjoyed the "*Addobbo*" prosciutto!

He enjoyed it fully! The way it was sliced, the right amount of fat, the very delicate almond flavour of the meat and the way it melted in his mouth!

I think that Mario made someone happy!

Luciano with Cora and Jeremy.

Intelligence at Work!

The parents and two young children stop by looking with curiosity at what I am doing.

I start to explain to them that I roast chestnuts...Chestnuts! The parents are not interested in the process, they are interested in the "chestnuts." I start to explain to them the "Chestnut culture..." The children are looking with great interest at what I am doing. I suggest the father pick up the smaller one in his arm so that he can see better the whole process. He takes him into his arms and now the children are all looking with great attention and interest.

The girl, a bit bigger, is looking through the front grill, and is very attentive too.

I explain to the parents that I am a lucky grandfather and that I know the way children look. I call it "intelligence at work!" That's because the eyes are the windows of the soul and it is by looking that children learn everything in life.

I usually end my sentence by saying to the parents: "Don't teach, learn from them!

A Slice of Sweet Bread

I took the *fornella* outside and went inside to get my double espresso from Zach.

When I went out again, there, all wrapped up, was a slice of sweet bread with raisins, nuts and other delicacies.

What a surprise! It goes well with my double espresso!

I started to savour it! And a sip of espresso.

What a delight!

What a way to start the day!

Raymond comes out.

"Oh! You found it! My wife made it and sent it to you!"

"Well, now it tastes even better! "

But I did not tell this to my friend Raymond.

A Sweet Surprise!

He is very friendly. He is Swiss. He is a customer. He came to me with a piece of gingerbread that his mother had made:

"Here, taste it, my mother made it back in Switzerland. She makes it every four months and she sends it to me. Let me know how you like it. Tomorrow I will be going skating on the canal and I will pass by afterwards for some chestnuts."

The following day he came by again.

"How was it?"

"Unique!" I answered. I could not say anything else. Indeed it had a unique taste.

"Thank you. Glad you liked it. I will bring you some more."

Later on in the day he came by again with some more "special gingerbread." I took it home and I shared it with some friends. They agreed with me that it had a unique taste!

Pizzelle!

Ida è venuta, come ogni settimana, a fare la spesa a "La Bottega."
"Ciao, come va? Mi fa piacere vederti. Dov'eri la settimana scorsa? Non ti ho visto. Ti avevo portato un dolcetto. Ho dovuto riportarlo a casa."
Ida non mi dà nemmeno il tempo di rispondere....
"Ecco qua, oggi ti ho portato qualcos'altro ma stai attento di non romperlo, è molto fragile. Tienilo così!"
E mi dà in mano un sacchetto.
Le do delle castagne....
"No! No! Sono troppe! Dammene solo qualcuna..."
La servo. Metto gentilmente da parte il sachetto che Ida mi ha dato, e continuo il mio lavoro.
Alla fine della giornata prendo il sachetto e me ne ritorno a casa.
Avevamo degli ospiti per cena alla fine della quale ho aperto il sachetto e, sorpresa! Il sachetto era pieno di "pizzelle abbruzzesi" freschissime, delicatamente saporite al limone, si scioglievano in bocca.
Tutti siamo stati molto soddisfatti di questo regalo inaspettato, tanto è vero che quelle che restarono.....le abbiamo offerte ai nostri ospiti da portare a casa. Le hanno accettate con molto piacere!

Pizzelle

There she is, like every weekend, Ida comes to shop at "La Bottega."
"Ciao, how are you? It is a pleasure to see you. Where were you last week? I did not see you! I brought you a cake. I had to take it back home."
She did not give me the time to answer ...
"Here, today I brought you something also, but be careful. Don't break it! It is very fragile! Keep it like this!" And she gives me a bag. I give her some chestnuts....
"No! No! They are too many! Give me only a few..."
I serve her. I gently put aside the bag that Ida gave me and I continue with my work

At the end of the day I took the bag home.

We had some guests for supper and at the end of it I opened the bag and, surprise! The bag was full of freshly made "pizzelle abbruzzesi!" very fresh, of a very delicate lemon flavour, that simply melted in the mouth.

Everyone was very delighted with the unexpected gift. It was so appreciated by our guests that they took home the rest!

Lou's Boots

He passes by every day.

"Hello."

"Hello."

One day I met him at Loblaws on College Square.

"What are you doing here?" He asked me.

"I am buying chicken for my homemade chicken soup." I told him.

When I saw him in the Market I asked him:

"What were you doing at Loblaws?"

"I live closeby."

"What are you doing here in the Market?"

"I own 'Lou's Boots.'"

"Oh, I see. A good friend of mine and his wife just bought two pairs of boots at your store. They are very happy."

"I am glad." He said smiling.

Thanks for Doing This!

Sometimes I think that I should not do this anymore but profit is not the reason for me to roast chestnuts! If we consider all the time and expenses I have it may not be worth doing it.

He approached me.

"Can I have a bag please?"

I served him.

While leaving he said:

"Thank you for doing this!"

He made my presence in the Market worthwhile!

A Book a Day!

It is incredible the interaction I have every day! Every hour! Every minute! While I was thinking this I thought that I had enough material to write a book a day!

La comunità italiana di Ottawa

Amo la comunità italiana di Ottawa. Amo farne parte e ad ogni occasione che si presenta sono disponibile per promuovere la cultura ed i valori della nostra comunità.

Capita spesso che ci siano delle attività culturali e sociali alle quali mi fa molto piacere partecipare e contribuire nella migliore maniera possibile.

Il quattro novembre si celebra la Festa Nazionale dell'Unità d'Italia e delle Forze Armate.

Organizzata da Angelo Filoso, Presidente dell'Italian Canadian Community Center, il quattro novembre 2012, c'è stata una bellissima cerimonia con la celebrazione di una messa solenne, sfilata di bandiere, bande della Polizia e dei Pompieri di Ottawa, con la partecipazione di S.E. Meloni, Ambasciatore d' Italia in Ottawa, e di una grande folla. Faceva freddo ma tutti sono rimasti sino alla fine della cerimonia durante la quale hanno suonato il "silenzio" ed hanno deposto ghirlande di fiori al monumento dei caduti eretto in Piazza Dante proprio davanti alla Chesa di Sant' Antonio.

Qualche giorno prima, Angelo Filoso mi aveva chiesto se ero disponibile per servire delle caldarroste ai presenti alla Festa. Ho detto di sì senza esitare. Ed il quattro novembre ero là, in Piazza Dante, ben presto al mattino a prepararmi per arrostire castagne.

A cerimonia finita, Rina Filoso e Lena Buffone si sono messe a fianco alla fornella per distribuire le caldarroste. Tre ciascuno, per cominciare.

Abbiamo colto tutti di sorpresa. Caldarroste? *Roasted chestnuts?* Incredibile! Non ci credevano!

Rina e Lena a volte sono state molto popolari durante la distribuzione delle castagne...Naturalmente c'erano quelli e quelle che ne volevano qualcuna in più... Naturalmente! Erano così buone!

Una volta finito di distribuirne a tutti ce ne sono rimaste parecchie. Rina e Lena si sono fatte premura di portarle subito nel sottosuolo della chiesa dove veniva servito un rinfresco. È inutile dire che le castagne sono state "le preferite" di tutto il "ben di Dio" che c'era sulle tavole!

The Italian Community of Ottawa

I love the Italian community of Ottawa. I love being part of it and at every occasion that presents itself to me I make myself available to promote the culture and the values of our community.

It occurs very often that there are social and cultural activities in which I participate with pleasure and contribute in the best way I possibly can.

On November 4th we celebrate the Italian National Unity and the Italian Armed Forces.

Organized by Angelo Filoso, President of the Italian Community Center, there was a beautiful ceremony on November 4th with a solemn mass, parade of flags of the different Associations, the Police and the Firefighters bands of Ottawa. Also present were H.E. Meloni the Italian Ambassador in Canada, and a very large crowd. It was cold but the people stayed until the end of the ceremony during which they played the Canadian and the Italian National Anthems, and they laid the wreaths at the monument of the fallen soldiers in Piazza Dante, in front of Saint Anthony's Church

A few days earlier, Angelo Filoso asked me if I was available to serve some roasted chestnuts to the people present at the celebration. I accepted without hesitation and on November 4th I was there, in Piazza Dante, early in the morning getting ready to roast chestnuts.

Once the ceremony ended, Rina Filoso and Lena Buffone came beside the *fornella* to begin distributing the freshly roasted chestnuts, three to each person.

We surprised everyone. *Caldarroste?* Roasted chestnuts? Incredible! They couldn't believe it!

Rina e Lena, sometimes were very popular during the distribution of the chestnuts....Naturally there were those who wanted a few more...Naturally! They were so good! Once everyone had had his/her share, there were a lot of chestnuts left over. Rina and Lena hurried to take them to the church basement were everybody gathered for coffee and cookies. Needless to say the chestnuts were the favorite besides everything else that was also on the tables!

Villa Marconi

L'ultima attività della stagione quest'anno l'ho riservata per i residenti di Villa Marconi, la Casa di Riposo per gli Italo-Canadesi di Ottawa.

Per me questo è un avvenimento speciale perché a me piace molto offrire qualche minuto di attivià differente ai residenti di Villa Marconi. Devo anche dire che sono particolarmente dedicato a Villa Marconi perché durante l'estate mi occupo di fare l'orto che è ben apprezzato dai residenti e da chi li visita.

Eccomi allora nel pomeriggio del 27 febbraio a Villa Marconi per prepararmi a servire le caldarroste verso le 6:30 di sera.

Quel giorno infuriava una terribile bufera di neve su Ottawa. Mi sono sistemato per bene sotto il portico e ho cominciato a preparare le castagne che fortunatamente erano ancora di buona qualità anche se erano un po' asciutte.

Verso le 6:30 gli addetti hanno portato una ventina di residenti nell'entrata principale. Le caldarroste erano pronte e ben stufate. I volontari le hanno pelate e subito servite calde hai residenti che pian piano le hanno gustate.

Mentre osservavo il tutto mi chiedevo quanti ricordi quelle caldarroste avranno suscitato in quelle persone anziane!

Tele-30, il canale della televisione di Rogers che trasmette il programma televisivo italiano era là a raccogliere testimonianze, sentimenti e ricordi dei residenti e dei volontari!

È già il terzo anno che faccio questa attività per i residenti di Villa Marconi e credo che la mia stagione di castagnaro non sarebbe completa se alla fine non ci fosse questo evento.

Villa Marconi

The last activity this year I reserved for the residents of Villa Marconi, the home for the Italian- Canadian seniors of Ottawa.

For me this is a very special event because I love to offer something different to the residents of Villa Marconi. I must say that I am particularly dedicated to Villa Marconi because during the summer I take care of the vegetable garden that is very appreciated by the residents and the visitors.

So, here I am, on the afternoon of February 27, at Villa Marconi getting ready to serve the freshly roasted chestnuts at 6:30 p.m.

That day there was a terrible snowstorm over Ottawa. I was well set up and well-protected on the back porch and I started to prepare the chestnuts that were a bit dry but still of good quality. Around 6:30 some volunteers and staff brought twenty residents to the main lobby. The chestnuts were well- roasted and stewed, ready to be eaten. The volunteers peeled them and, while still warm, they served the residents who very slowly savored and enjoyed them.

While I was observing the whole scene I was asking myself how many memories those chestnuts were stirring in those seniors.

Tele-30, the Rogers channel that broadcasts the Italian television program was there to capture the sentiments and memories of the residents, of the family members, and of the volunteers.

It is the third year that I do this activity for the residents of Villa Marconi. I believe that the chestnut roasting season would not be complete if this event did not take place.

First Sunny Day

March 9, 2013, the first sunny weekend in Ottawa, Paolo and I went for a car ride in different parts of the city and we stopped at the Rockcliffe Lookout. The sun was beautiful and warm, the Gatineau and Ottawa Rivers were still frozen. We enjoyed the view.

A young lady was seated on the floor of the Lookout, reading. Paolo went to get the camera in the car and started to take some photos. While he was taking photos the young lady got up and sat on the railing of the Lookout. Jokingly I said to her: "Be careful not to fall down."

Well, this was the beginning of a very nice conversation. Agathe, works on art restoration and she remembered me as the chestnut roaster guy. We kept talking, in French, English and Italian. She studied in Turin for two years. Isn't it a small world! Ah! The "power of the chestnut connection!"

After Rockcliffe we went to the ByWard Market. It was invaded by people enjoying the sunny day. I stopped to say hello to the people I knew and, when passing by Sheila, the jeweler artist in the artisan section of the Byward building, I opened the door to say "Hi!" to her. She was busy with a lady customer. As soon as she saw me she said:

"Hi Luciano! I miss you!"

"I miss you too!" I replied.

The lady customer looked at her, looked at me, they smiled, they smiled again at the unexpected, surprising act of friendship.

Three Cellphones

It was a very nice winter day in Ottawa at the ByWard Market.

Here I am enjoying the roasting of chestnuts, selling them, interacting with people.

A moment of calm. I look at the chestnuts roasting. It was a pleasant, beautiful moment.

I lift my eyes and, on the sidewalk in front of me, passing by, in different directions, with different attitudes were three people with their cellphone to their ear, talking, listening, without paying attention to the Market's environmental "energy" of things to do, to see....

For a moment my past profession of building superintendent emerged. I stopped thinking about roasting chestnuts and I thought about all the energy those cellphones use, about all the computer rooms kept functioning 24/7/365. Those computer rooms need air conditioning, ventilation, alarms, mechanical and electrical systems, operators, buildings, rooms, etc. And all those requirements are needed around the clock.

Around the world! In every country! Incredible!

All those electronic waves are going through buildings, people, children...

What are and what will the consequences be?

How energy safe is this huge system?

What a powerful machine mankind has created! And yet how vulnerable the whole system is for we depend on it so much!

What can I do? I asked myself.

Nothing. I am a victim like everyone else.

I kept roasting chestnuts.

Brian

Brian Lavergne is my personal computer technician.

Sorry, let's rephrase it. Brian is my personal friend and he also services my personal computer. He has serviced my computer ever since I bought it from him a few years ago.

This morning I took my computer into his shop "Silicon Valley Computer Systems," for a cleanup and also to get some answers to some questions on how certain functions of the PC work. Brian teaches me also how to use special features of the PC.

But, you might ask what do computers, PC's and all this modern technology have to do with chestnuts?

Read on please....

Here I am, in the afternoon to pick up the computer serviced and ready to go. Brian is cleaning it meticulously with a brush while he answers some of my questions. Once he has given me all the answers, looking at me, he adds:

"My son and his wife went to see you at the Market and they bought some freshly roasted chestnuts from you. They found them delicious! Kathy, Adam's wife, mentioned that you were a very nice man and that you are very knowledgeable about chestnuts. They spent about 15 minutes talking with you and went away feeling wonderful. You really made their day."

'Well...'' I answered."I thank you for these nice and unexpected comments. It is a small world, isn't it? Whoever expected that your son and his wife would have enjoyed 'freshly roasted chestnuts, flavor and culture!'" .

"How much do I owe you for your services today?"

"Nothing." Said Brian.

"Thank you, Brian. Tell Adam and Kathy to pass by on the weekend. I will give them some freshly roasted chestnuts for free!"

That's another nice and unexpected experience!

Jim

Here I was tending to my favourite pastime, roasting chestnuts in Ottawa's ByWard Market. It was a very cold day, ideal for the first day of Winterlude in Canada's National Capital. On the other side of George Street the ByWard Market authorities had put up a big tent. They were having a "Stew Cook-Off contest," all proceeds going to charity. That day I sent several of my friends and customers to this event. They enjoyed the idea, the event and the stew.

I look around and there he is!

"Hi, Jim! How are you?"

Jim, Mr. Jim Watson, the Mayor of Ottawa, in person, with his assistant, were walking by me.

"Can I offer you some chestnuts?" I asked them.

They came near me.

"No, thank you. We enjoyed some very good stew. We are fine now."

I said to his assistant:

"Mr. Watson told me to call him Jim. I hold him in regard both as a person and as the Mayor of Ottawa!"

"No problem," the assistant replied.

Mr. Watson asked me:

"So, will you be roasting chestnuts during Winterlude? You are going to be our Ambassador for the visitors that are coming to Ottawa!"

"I will do my best."

I could not keep them any longer. They had to go back to City Hall. It was cold, and they were walking.

What a pleasant surprise! It made my day.

Pappardelle all'anatra

John is a great chef and a great friend of mine.

Late one afternoon he passed by to say "hello." I gave him some chestnuts.

He was going home to prepare supper for himself and his girlfriend, maybe some fresh chicken that he would buy on the way home and prepare while he waited for her to come home.

"Why don't you prepare her some 'Pappardelle all'anatra — pasta with duck!" I suggested to him. "Here in Canada we have the best duck in the world, 'Les Canards de Bromond.' Duck is very healthy, the fat is good and there is no cholesterol. This was the favorite meal of the Gondoliers in Venice: 'Pasta all'anatra!'"

I convinced him that, on the way home, instead of chicken John should buy a fresh duck right here in the ByWard Market. He could season it, roast it in the oven, cover it in a casserole with white wine, onions, rosemary, salt, pepper and sage.

35-40 minutes after the duck was roasted, he should take the meat and strain the sauce and set it aside.

Boil the bones, strain the broth, and in the broth cook the *pappardelle*. Once cooked, add the duck meat and the sauce. White wine is strongly recommended!

He did it.

She loved it! And now she loves John even more.

Recipe:

Take a duck and inside the cavity put some fresh sage leaves, rosemary, a peeled onion cut in 4 pieces, salt, pepper and an orange peel.

Sprinkle salt and pepper on the outside, add some sage leaves and place it in a cooking pot and down with a grill under so it does not bake on the fat that it will release.

Add some white wine in the pot, cover the pot well so that the vapour does not escape and put it in the oven pre-heated at 300F.

After half an hour turn it and baste the top and the inside with the liquid that it has produced. Cover it againl and place it in the oven for another half hour or until the meat detaches easily form the bones. Once the duck has cooled off remove the meat and some lean skin; cut it in small pieces and add it to the previously strained sauce in the pot. Add some chopped parsley.

Take the bones, the skin and all the sesonings. Put them in a pot, add cold water and boil it for about an hour. Strain it while warm so that the fat remains with the broth.

Take the pappardelle *pasta (wide noodels), and cook it in the duck broth where you have previously added salt. Cook it "al dente." Strain it, put it in a frying pan, add some cooking water, some duck sauce with meat, parmesan cheese, and parsely. Stir it, put it in a serving dish, add some duck and meat sauce on top and serve it with parmesan cheese.*

Pesto rosso:
Take some sun dried tomatoes with their oil, garlic, fresh basil; add some olive oil and blend them until smooth. Taste it, and if it is too acidic, add some maple syrup to taste. Serve it with crostini.

Ernestina

During this time many people came to see me and all of them had the same question:
"No chestnuts, today?"
Once they knew my answer they were very disappointed.
One gentleman returned four times hoping that there was a "yes" answer. He and his wife were entertaining people from out of town that evening and they were hoping to surprise them with some freshly roasted chestnuts.
Ernestina, an elderly friend of mine, came by to shop at "La Bottega." She asked me for roasted chestnuts.
"Sorry." I replied.
She was very disappointed so I gave her some of mine, cut and ready to be roasted. She had no words to thank me. She went into "La Bottega" to do her shopping. When she came out she gave me a package of *Lavazza* espresso coffee.
"Here." She said. "Enjoy it with your wife."
Another lady came by. She gave me a pair of thermal socks from Mark's Men's wear. I couldn't give her anything in return.
A family came by.
"No chestnuts? We came all the way from Peterborough for you..."
"I am sorry." I replied.
In the afternoon two ladies stopped in front of me, looking at me, staring at me...
"No chestnuts?"
"Sorry."
"We came from Montreal. We are staying at The Lord Elgin

Hotel, and we came to Ottawa to see you, to have a photo taken with you," said Anne showing me the disposable camera she had bought here in Ottawa for the occasion.

"I am very sorry." I repeated.

Having said that I invited Ann and Hélène to have a cappuccino at "La Bottega" before calling a taxi to take them to the train station and head back to Montreal very, very disappointed. I could tell you many more of these touching stories that I live with every day, but I cannot continue.

François, le "madonnaro"

François est un 'madonnaro' (peintre de Vierges), un peintre de rue, un de ces artistes que créé des œuvres artistiques sur la rue William, entre les rues Rideau et George.

Lorsque la température est clémente, il est là tôt le matin jusqu'à tard le soir. François aime son travail. Plusieurs admirent et apprécient la façon dont il s'exprime à travers son art avec des craies de différentes couleurs. Je considère François comme un grand ami. Merci François pour tous les gens que tu rends heureux.

Me voici encore un autre jour au Marché, rencontrant des gens, socialisant, discutant, et pourquoi pas, en faisant des affaires. Voilà. Je pense que François vient me voir. Il vient de tourner le coin des rues William et Georges et vient vers moi.

"Qui est le prochain?" J'ai continué à servir les clients.

François m'a approché mais j'étais trop occupé. Je lui ai montré les sacs de marrons qui étaient prêts à la vente. Il a commencé à les vendre aux clients. Il sait comment faire, et il m'aide toujours lorsqu'il vient aux alentours.

Entre deux clients, je lui demande comment il va.

"Je suis allé voir Hector…"

"Hector? Je pensais que je connaissais tous tes amis, comme tu connais tous les miens."

Nous parlions pendant que je faisais rôtir les marrons et qu'il les vendait aux clients.

"Hector est un ami spécial. Il me tient compagnie. Il me parle l'été pendant que je peint ici dans le Marché. Et maintenant, il est là, seul."

"Hector, seul?"

"Oui, Hector, sous le chêne rouge. C'est là que je peins l'été".

"Ah, je comprends…"

"Un sac de marrons? François va vous servir aujourd'hui". "Hector me parle lorsque la brise souffle sur les feuilles. Il me protège avec son ombre de cette bruine qui autrement ruinerait mes travaux. Il me tient compagnie quand personne est là". François devient très émotif.

"Je suis allé voir comment il a affronté la grande chute de neige hier soir".

"Comment a-t-il résisté?"

"Très bien. Les feuilles sont encore couvertes de neige, mais, c'est un chêne, et les chênes sont forts. Il va survivre à l'hiver comme il l'a fait pour les dix sept dernières années, depuis quezj'ai commencé à peindre sous lui".

"Intéressant" lui dis-je. "Les marronniers et les chênes sont de la même famille d'arbres, alors si les chênes survivent, les marronniers aussi survivront". On ne cesse jamais d'apprendre dans la vie.

"Hum!...Je me demande si il va survivre…"

"Que veux-tu dire?" Je le demande intrigué.

"La grille en fer forgé autour de son pied l'étouffe".

"Quoi? J'ai besoin de voir cela".

À la fin de ma journée, je suis allé voir Hector. La grille en fer forgé était en effet incrustée dans son tronc. Avec le temps, Hector, dans sa croissance, avait en effet couvert la grille de fer. Le lendemain, j'ai appelé 311, le numéro de la ville et j'ai expliqué la situation. Ils m'ont donné un numéro de rapport.

Quelques jours se sont passés. Un employé de la ville m'a appelé pour me dire qu'ils avaient retiré la grille. J'en étais heureux.

Hector était sauvé.

J'ai appelé François et je lui ai dit que son ami Hector était sauvé.

François, the **madonnaro**

François is a *madonnaro*, a street painter, one of those artists that create beautiful works on William Street between Rideau and George street. Time permitting he is there early in the morning until late at night. François is very happy with his work. Many people admire and appreciate the way he expresses himself in his art with chalk of different colours. I consider François a great friend of mine. Thank you François for all the people you make happy.

Here I am another day at the Market meeting many people, socializing, talking, and why not, doing some business.

There. I think François is coming to see me. He just turned the corner of William and George Streets and is coming towards me.

"Who's next?" I kept on serving the clients.

François approached me but I was too busy. I indicated to him the bags of chestnuts that were ready to be sold. He started to sell them to the customers right away. He knows how to do it, and he always helps me when he comes around.

Between clients I ask how he is doing.

"I went to see Hector...."

"Hector? I thought I knew all your friends, like you know all mine."

We were talking while I was roasting chestnuts and he was

selling them to the clients.

"Hector is a special friend. He keeps me company. He talks to me during the summer when I paint here in the Market. And now he is there, lonely."

"Hector, lonely?"

"Yes, Hector, under the red oak tree. That's where I paint in the summer."

"Oh! I understand..."

"One bag of chestnuts? François will serve you today."

"Hector talks to me when the breeze moves the leaves. He protects me with his shadow from that misty rain that otherwise ruins my work. He keeps me company when no one is around."

François becomes very emotional.

"I went to see how he handled last night's heavy snowfall."

"How he handled it?"

"Very well. The leaves are still covered with snow, but he is an oak tree and they are strong. He will survive the winter like he has done for the past seventeen years since I started painting under him."

"Interesting," I said. "Chestnut trees are of the same family as oak trees, so if the oak trees survive, chestnut trees will also survive." We can never stop learning in this life.

"Hum!...I wonder if it will survive..."

"What do you mean?" I asked him, puzzled.

"The cast iron grate around Hector's base is choking it."

"What? I have to see this."

At the end of my day I went to see Hector. The cast iron grate was indeed into its trunk because over time Hector had overgrown the hole in the cast iron grate.

The next day I called 311, the City number, and I explained the case. They gave me a report number.

A coupe of days went by. A city employ called me to tell me that they had removed the grate. I was happy.

Hector was safe.

I called François and told him that his fried Hector was safe.

Charcoal

I roast the chestnuts with wood charcoal that I buy at Canadian Tire on Merivale and Hunt Club. Why do I mention the store in the chronicles?

Because one day, early in the season, I went there to buy a good supply of wood charcoal. I had 6-8 bags of coal in the cart. I was with Greg A. We met an employee who looked at us as if to ask,

"What are you doing with all that charcoal?"

I stopped and asked him:

"Can you provide me with a supply of charcoal during the winter? I need it to roast chestnuts."

"To roast chestnuts?"

And here I am explaining to the employee the roasting of chestnuts technique, culture and profession and, most importantly, why I need wood charcoal and not any other coal for better tasting chestnuts. He was very attentive and friendly. At the end of the conversation I asked if he, or the manager could guarantee me a supply of wood charcoal for the whole winter

"I am Brad, the store manager and I will make sure that we will have a supply of this particular wood charcoal all Winter!"

He kept his promise.

One day Greg A. suggested to me to bring a basket of roasted chestnuts to the store to surprise and thank Brad for his kindness and cooperation.

I prepared a nice basket of freshly roasted chestnuts and took it to the store. I went to the service desk and gave it to the lady:

"These are roasted chestnuts. Please give them to Brad, the store manager. It's a surprise!"

Later on in the season I met Brad in the store. His face lit up. "Thank you, Luciano, for the chestnuts. What a surprise! I took the basket to the lunchroom so that all the employees could taste them. They loved them. Thank you!"

Remembrance Day

On Sunday Nov. 11, I was roasting chesnuts when at 11 o' clock I heard gun shots on Parliament Hill.

I stopped what I was doing out of respect for the fallen soldiers.

I know about the First World War. The last gun shots were fired in my own town, Vittorio Veneto. The holes are still there, on a building in Via Roma.

After the ceremony a lot of people came to the Market. I promised myself to offer freshly roasted chestnuts to all the people in uniform and to all the veterans.

So I did. They accepted and enjoyed them.

A frail veteran tasted half of a chestnut with his eyes closed… Where did the flavour of the chestnut take him? Maybe to some battlefield or maybe to some forest? Who knows? One thing I know for sure is that we were all looking at him and travelling with his feelings and emotions….

Elderly Man

December 29.

Today it snowed constantly. A family came around and dropped off their elderly father. The elderly mother and a daughter went shopping. The father, there, in front of me, was admiring the snow falling and the ByWard Market's activity. He took out a handkerchief to blow his nose. A gust of wind blew the handkerchief away and the elderly man bent down to try to pick it up. He lost his balance, but walking forward tried to regain it. Impossible!...I ran toward him. Just a fraction of a second before he stepped off the sidewalk and into the street he miraculously regained control of his balance.

I was so relieved!

In my mind I pictured the frightening scene of the elderly man run over by a speeding car right there on George Street in the ByWard Market!

A Word of Thanks

Because of the snow I took shelter in front of 60 George St. A man came to see me. He bought some freshly roasted chestnuts and, before leaving, he said:
"Thank you for being here!"
Another customer said:
"You are doing a great job. Thank you!"

Asian Man

An Asian man came around. He had an old Roley Flex camera. We talked about cameras. I told him that I had a Zeiss Super Iconta many years ago. He said that the Rolley Flex he had was made in 1929 and he was taking photos to be published on the net about "The streets of Ottawa". He asked me to pose for him with some roasted chestnuts!

Constables

They always pass by me at the beginning of their shift.
Today there are two teams of two police officers. The first team is made up of two ladies. A few minutes later the usual two police officers pass by. They stop briefly to chat, to ask me how my day is going and to wish me a "Happy New Year."
I could not stop thinking how much I respect them. I respect them as persons, as friends, as law officers, and as simple workers who have to leave their families to serve our society.
I had to leave the cart for a few seconds, and one of the officer said:
"Go head, I will look after the cart! Service to society!"

Vincenzo

Lo vedo da lontano che sta arrivando: ben vestito, ordinato, va piano, guarda in giro. A me sembra che apprezzi molto il suo tempo di svago. È pensionato e vive in un appartamento vicino alla "piccola Italia" di Ottawa. Vincenzo ha l'abbonamento mensile per viaggiare con l'autobus. Quando decide di uscire prende l'autobus, va al "Caffè Cosenza" su Preston Street, beve un caffè, e, se trova, fa una chiaccherata con gli amici e poi riprende l'autobus per venire al Mercato a comperare i giornali.

Vincenzo è di origine siciliana e mi racconta che ha viaggiato in tutto il mondo. Quando era giovane faceva il meccanico nelle sale motori delle grandi navi che solcavano gli oceani. Mentre mi racconta i suoi viaggi non posso fare a meno d'invidiarlo!

Da una parte.

Dall'altra non so se lo invidio veramente perché non riesco ad immaginarmi di lavorare per ore ed ore chiuso nella stiva di una nave, con i rumori dei motori, il calore, l'umidità...Meglio che non ci pensi.

Vincenzo entra ne "La Bottega" e qualche minuto dopo esce con la borsa della spesa.

"Cosa hai comperato?" Gli chiedo.

"Ho trovato questo olio d'oliva in svendita," mi risponde mostrandomi una bottiglia d'olio d'oliva extra vergine.

"Buonissimo! Come lo adoperi?"

"Non lo so, vedrò."

"Ti spiego io come adoperarlo. Lo adoperi crudo versandone un filo sulle insalate, le paste, la carne già cotta, sui risotti, su tutti i piatti e pietanze prima di mangiarli."

Mi guarda stupito.

"Crudo, così...Non l'avevo mai sentito...."

Altri due anziani amici italiani si avvicinano.

"Ciao Vincenzo, come va?"

"Va bene, ma ora devo andare a vedere se sono arrivati i miei giornali. Arrivederci...."

Ed è così che Vincenzo se ne va. Credo che ci sia qualche divergenza tra di loro.

Poco dopo Vincenzo torna ed allora mi spiega tutte le versioni di come interpretare la politica, in particolare quella italiana......

Vincent

I see him from far away coming towards me slowly, well dressed, neat, as he looks around. It seems to me that he appreciates his freedom a lot. He is retired and he lives in an apartment near Ottawa's "Little Italy." Vincent has a monthly bus pass. He can ride the bus, any bus, at any time. When he decides to go out he takes the bus and he goes to "Caffè Cosenza" on Preston Street. He has his espresso and, if he find the right company, he socializes and then takes the bus to come to the Market and buy the newspapers.

Vincent is from Sicily and he tells me that he travelled all over the world. When he was young he was a mechanic in the motor rooms of the big ships that crossed the oceans. While he was telling me his travel experiences I could not help but envy him.

But, on the other hand, I don't think I will envy him too much because I cannot think of myself working for hours in an engine room with the noise of the motors, the heat, the humidity, the smell...

Better not to think about it!

Vincent enters "La Bottega" and a few minutes later comes out with a shopping bag.

"What did you buy?" I ask.

"I found this olive oil on special" and he shows me a bottle of extra virgin olive oil.

"Very good oil! How do you use it?"

"I don't know, I will see."

" I tell you how to use it: use it directly, just a little bit on salads, cooked meat, risotto and you can even put some on every dish that is ready to be eaten."

Vincent looks at me with curiosity.

"Straight, like this?...I never heard of it..."

Two other Italians friends are approaching us.

"Ciao, Vincenzo, how are you?"

"I am doing fine, but now I have to go and see if my newspapers have arrived. See you....."

There, Vincent leaves us. I believe there is something going on between them...

Few minutes later Vincent is back and he explains to me the many ways to interpret politics, especially Italian politics...

L'altro Vincenzo

Questo Vincenzo lo puoi incontrare un po' da per tutto in Ottawa: semplice, simpatico, ama conversare e socializzare con chiunque. Più che ottantenne viaggia ovunque in autobus e a piedi, gode la sua vita stando fuori di casa. È così che vive! Lo incontro spesso nei caffè, nei negozi, per la strada, e a "La Bottega."

Un giorno mi racconta che era appena ritornato dalla sua Campania natale e, data la sua età avanzata, mi confida che forse questa sarà la sua ultima visita all'amata Italia. Sempre parlando e sapendo la mia passione per le castagne, mi dice che ne ha portate alcune che lui stesso ha raccolto nelle colline vicinanti dove abitava.

"Potresti darmene qualcuna?" Gli chiedo, "Portamele a casa, lo sai dove abito!"

"Sì, lo so, te le porto."

Quanche giorno dopo qualcuno suona alla porta, apro, eccolo là davanti a me con un sachetto di plastica in mano con qualche castagna dentro. Lo invito ad entrare. No, non vuole entrare. Mi ha portato otto castagne come promesso…Me ne ero quasi scordato!

Le ho piantate nei vasetti di terracotta che custodisco gelosamente in casa. Cinque stanno già germogliando. Quando riterrò opportuno inviterò Vincenzo al loro battesimo.

The Other Vincent

You can bump into this Vincent almost anywhere in Ottawa: he is simple, affable, loves to talk and to interact with anyone. He is more than eighty years old and travels everywhere by bus and on foot. He enjoys life by being outside his house. That's how he lives.

I often meet him in coffee shops, stores, in the streets and at "La Bottega."

One day he tells me that he has just returned from his native Campania, and, he confides, that, because of his age, this may be his last trip to his beloved Italy. While talking, and knowing my passion for chestnuts, he tells me that he has brought some over that he himself picked on the hills near where he lived. "Could you give me some?" I ask him. "Bring them to my place, you know where I live." "Yes, I know. I will bring them." A few days later someone rings the bell. I open the door, and there he is in front of me with a plastic bag in his hand containing some chestnuts. I ask him to come in. He refuses. He brought me eight chestnuts as he had promised. I had almost forgotten about it.

I planted them in the clay vases I guard in my house. Five are already sprouting. When I think it's the right time I will invite Vincent for their baptism.

Gesto di convivialità

Rinaldo è uno dei più rinomati parrucchieri per signora in Ottawa. Lo conosco da parecchi anni, da quando esercitavo ancora la professione di "Stationary Engineer." Rinaldo si avvicina mentre arrostisco castagne, socializziamo. Ad un tratto una bella e grossa castagna ci sorride, la buccia si è aperta facendo vedere la castagna bella cotta con i zuccheri delicatamente caramellati in maniera uniforme. La guardo, l'ammiro, la indico a Rinaldo.

"Ti sorride," gli dico.

Rinaldo allunga la mano e prende la castagna bella calda!

Questo semplice gesto di convivialità mi ha molto toccato. L'ho ancora fisso nella mente e quando trovo la persona con la dovuta personalità non posso fare a meno di suggerirgli di ripetere il gesto che ha fatto Rinaldo. Infallibilmente ho da tutti questo bellissimo ed apprezatissimo gesto di convivialità che a me piace moltissimo!

A Gesture of Conviviality

Rinaldo is one of the most famous hairdressers in Ottawa. I have known him for many years, since I was still working as "Stationary Engineer." Rinaldo approaches me as I am roasting chestnuts. We start talking. Suddenly a big beautiful chestnut smiles at us. The rind had opened showing the chestnut roasted to perfection with the sugars uniformly golden. I look at it, I admire it, I point it to Rinaldo.

"It's smiling at you." I say.

Rinaldo extends his hand and picks up the hot chestnut. This simple gesture of conviviality touched me. It's still fixed in my mind. And when I come across a person with the right personality I can't help but suggest to him to make the same gesture as Rinaldo's. Always, everyone makes this most beautiful and appreciated gesture of conviviality that I like very much.

Bicycles vs Cars!

A bicycle tied to the bicycle post in front of me attracted my attention. It was beautiful and it looked expensive. I took a good look. Indeed it was an expensive bike.

I could not help but think how the bicycle culture has evolved in my lifetime. My first new bicycle was a Bottecchia, it cost me $9.00 when I bought it new in my preteen years. A few days later someone stole it from me and I never saw it again.

While I was thinking about it a young lady approached the bike with her groceries. She had been shopping at "La Bottega." As she was arranging the grocery on the bike's baskets I said:.

"A beautiful and expensive bicycle, isn't it?"

"I decided to invest in a bicycle instead of investing in a car," she said.

"I love bicycles," I said. "I went with a group of Boy Scouts from Ottawa to Washington D.C. in 1987 cycle-camping. The year after we went around the Georgian Bay region. 1.800 kilometers. In 1990 we went to L'Ile de la Tortou, Haiti, to set up a bicycle repair shop for the local people."

I could have kept talking about my passion for bicycles for hours...

We could have kept talking of our passion for bicycles for hours!.....

"But nowadays we live in a "car society." I kept talking. "The bigger and more expensive the car is the more....."

"....aggressive the driver is!" She completed the sentence for me!

We were very much in tune with one another!

Skunks!

Angelo, my brother-in-law, is now retired and lives with his family on a farm an hour outside of Montréal. They invited us to spend New Year's Eve with them. While at the farm I mentioned to Angelo the episode about the bicycles versus cars. I did not finish as he said:

"Skunks!"

"What do you mean?" I asked him

"Did you ever ask yourself why there are so many skunks dead on the highways?"

"No." I said not knowing what Angelo was about to tell me.

"You see, skunks, when they sense danger, turn around and spray. They don't think about defending themselves in other ways like running away from danger. So are some of those drivers, they react! They don't think about the consequences!"

I could not agree more. Coming from Angelo it made very much sense. He is a retired biology professor. He taught biology all his life at a college in Montreal.

Chestnuts and Brussel Sprouts

When I got ready to go to the farm I prepared some chestnuts. I planned to roast them on the wood stove that they have at the farm house where they live year round. It is one of those big old stoves. It serves to cook meals and to heat the house at the same time.

So here I am, early in the morning, at the farm house, in the middle of nowhere. The temperature is -25-30C, a lot of snow all over, doing what I like best: roasting and peeling chestnuts!

While enjoying myself I was thinking that, once, back in time, this was my/our daily fall and winter breakfast....The voice of Lupe, my sister in law, brought me back to reality....

".....What a great idea!" She said. "For dinner today we will have a roast of moose and chestnuts with Brussel sprouts as a side dish! "

Accompanied by a good Amarone wine and good company, you cannot imagine how delicious that first New Year dinner was!

Recipe:

A dozen roasted chestnuts, peeled.
Two dozens Brussel sprouts
Half of a lemon peel
Butter, olive oil.
In a pan, with cover, put the olive oil and the butter, melt the butter, add the chestnuts, stir them slowly, lower the heat, cover.
In a pot bring some water to a boil, put the Brussel sprouts and the lemon peel in the boiling water. Boil the Brussel sprouts for 4-5 minutes, remove and put them in the pan with the chestnuts. Stir slowly, cover, put them aside for another 7-10 minutes stirring occasionally.
Season to personal taste
Serve them with roasted or grilled meat.

To *Culture (Cultivate)*
To Taste   (with Cheese!)

I have to say that when I prepare the chestnuts I find that a lot of them are sprouting, so I take them and I plant them.

I have a room with a southern exposure with a patio door that opens onto the backyard. I have a shelf and all that's necessary to plant and grow all sorts of plants and vegetables. I consider it a very important room.

Here they are, growing, what will become chestnuts trees!

I have them by the dozen. In late spring I plant them outside. I give them to friends so they can plant them. In the spring of 2012 I planted about 20 chestnut trees.

Ernie, from Grimo Nursery, sent me two chestnut tree that are the same as the ones that the Canadian Chestnut Council (CCC) plants. In 2011 the volunteers with the CCC planted 400 chestnut trees, and in 2012 they planted about 1.500 more. Why do they want to plant so many chestnut trees? Because chestnuts are good for human beings!

Just visit the site "Chestnuts Nutrition Facts" and you will be surprised to learn that chestnuts lower bad cholesterol while increasing the good one! They are high in vitamin C. They stabilize the red blood cells...

It happened to me. In 2010, during my annual routine checkup, the doctor found that my red blood cells count was low. He referred me to a specialist.

They took blood samples every month and indeed the red blood cells were getting lower and lower. But then I started the chestnut roasting season and by the end of January my red blood cells were fine! The specialist could not believe it!

"Why are they OK now?"

"It may depend on the chestnuts and the red wine!" I said with a smile

They took more tests and all was fine, so he dismissed me.

That's when I went on the web and found out about all the benefits of the chestnuts.

Now I realize why the Romans called the chestnuts the "bread from heaven, the bread of the poor!" I love chestnuts and cheese. I try them with a great variety of cheeses: Italian, French, etc. But I found that the perfect combination is between chestnuts and the six years old Perron Cheddar Cheese that they sell at "La Bottega." Just take a bit of Perron cheddar cheese and half of a roasted chestnut, chew them slowly and, well, indulge.

Now, have a sip of red wine with them.

Simply delicious!

The chestnuts were given to us by Mother Nature at the beginning of winter.

The chestnut trees grow in the mountains where human beings need more energy to survive the winter months!

Chestnuts are a cereal that can be easily conserved during the winter.

So, what better food is there than chestnuts?

Effective Coaching!

Right before Christmas I noticed that at "La Bottega" they were all very busy preparing and catering food. What surprised me the most was the way the employees were mentored, directed and supervised by Pat and Rocco. I really admire them.

After the holidays, during a quite moment in the store, I mentioned it to Rocco and congratulated both of them for their performance. He listened and, when I finished talking, he pointed to his coat.

I did not know what he meant. OK, it was an AC Milan coat.

"What do you mean?" I said.

"Effective coaching, that's what it is. We train our staff well, and when it is time to perform, they know what to do, just like the soccer players, first they train and then they perform on the field during a game!"

Joe from Rochester USA!

Joe is an Italo-American, born and raised in Rochester, New York. He has a stand at the local market where he sells the vegetable that he grows and other vegetables. He loves his profession and, like me, he loves to socialize and to have the responsibility to "report" to the customers every day. Yes, every day!

Joe loves and dreams of setting up a chestnut roasting stand like the one I have. Joe went on the web to get some information any information, just out of curiosity, and he found me! The chestnut roaster guy in Ottawa.

Joe phoned me:

"Has the season started? How is it going?....I would love to come and see you!" he said.

"Why don't you come up to Ottawa for the weekend?"

And here he is.

On Friday morning we are ready to go to the ByWard Market for our day of enjoyment! Joe, with his open personality, fitted right in, in no time! In minutes he became friends with every one at "La Bottega" and it did not take him too long to befriend all my customers. And he learned how to roast and serve chestnuts in no time.

Joe stayed at my place.We shared a couple of days together with my family. I also found time to show him the beauty of Ottawa and of the Region. He loved it! I believe he didn't want to leave. I think he would have liked to stay here, but he had to go back to his family, to his profession, to his farm.

Before he left, Joe bought a very good provision of olive oil

at "La Bottega," one bottle for his parents, one for his uncle, one for his friend, a few more to sell at the stand, in the market.....
When Joe was in Ottawa he took a lot of photos of the *fornella*, the roaster cart. When he got back to Rochester he applied for the license to roast chestnuts in the market. They never gave it to him!
Joe is still very disappointed.

John

John is retired now. He has time to enjoy the life that he likes best.
I don't remember how we met, but here we are now, roasting chestnuts together, in front of "La Bottega."
It is interesting how friendships can happen and get stronger day by day!
John and I have worked several weekends together. My customers were his customers. John enjoyed the experience of roasting chestnuts the same way I did, and still continue to do with joy!
I must say that John suggested some little ways to improve the art of roasting chestnuts. There are many fine and fun moments we share together.
Thank you, John.

Extended Culture

It is a great pleasure to promote the "Chestnut culture" in the Market, but I also have the pleasure of promoting it elsewhere. Take for example Nick, the owner of "La Favorita," one of my favorite restaurants in Ottawa's Little Italy. Nick loves chestnuts and I take every opportunity to provide him with some, and he is always very, very grateful!
I love to see him crack a fresh raw chestnut and then turn to me:
"They are good! Where did you buy them?"

Trattoria, Caffè Italia

Trattoria, in Italian, is a family run restaurant. At la "Trattoria Caffè Italia" in Ottawa's Little Italy, you feel that you are part of the Carozza family. Once you enter the "Trattoria Caffè Italia," Dominic, Pat, Connie, everyone, will make you feel at home.

One day I brought a basket of freshly roasted chestnuts there. When I arrived, I saw Hutch, a regular customer, seated at the bar counter. I approached him. I asked Salvatore, the bar tender, to give me a plate. I uncovered the chestnuts in the basket. Hutch looked at them very surprised!

"Chestnuts!" he said.

I took some out, put them in the plate and I handed them to him.

Surprised again! By the looks of it, for Hutch, it was love at first sight!

"Luciano," said Dominic, "my mother is here, she is in the back with Connie, can I bring her some chestnuts?"

"I will bring them to her," I said.

I took a few and I went in the back of the restaurant where Connie and her mother were seated. I put the plate of chestnuts on the table. The mother looked at them, ecstatic!

"Sono castagne, mamma," said Connie, and she started to peel one and give it to her mother to savour.

Somehow the mother's face changed to a happy expression. I could not resist. I gave her a kiss on her forehead, on her white hair. I left the mother and daughter reminiscing of the past, as they were enjoying the chestnuts!

I went back to the bar counter. Hutch was still seated with a glass of red wine in front of him, eating, savouring the chestnuts. Something was going on. Hutch looked different and seemed overcome with emotion.

I approached him. With tears in his eyes he started to talk, slowly.

"I remember when my mother used to prepare chestnuts for me and the rest of the family back in Germany when I was a little kid. Every morning we had a few chestnuts. That was our breakfast!"

While Hutch was talking, his emotions were getting more

and more visible. I could now see the feelings that Hutch was conveying to me so well, so naturally, with a such a friendly humanity that I could not remain indifferent.

I shared every emotion of Hutch's feelings and tears......!

Trattoria Caffè Italia

They meet often at "La Trattoria Caffè Italia" for lunch and every time they see me they ask:

"Dove sono le castagne?" Where are the chestnuts?"

One day I wanted to surprise them.

I roasted some chestnuts on my BBQ with a specially made pan. Once perfectly roasted I put them in a basket, well wrapped in a towel to keep them warm.

I arrived at "La Trattoria"as they were just finishing lunch. They asked me the usual question:

"Dove sono le castagne?"

I surprised them when I showed them the basket that was still steaming with a wonderful aroma of roasted chestnuts.

They pounced on them!

They were eating them as fast as they were peeling them. I had no reason to ask them if they liked them. They loved them!

Dominic Carozza was behind the counter doing something. I asked our friends to leave some for him. They assured me that they would.

A few minutes later Dominic came to the table where we were sitting and made space in the middle of the table for a beautiful cutting board filled with different cheeses, olives and other delicacies.

Dominic surprised me and every ones else at the table.

Dominic sat by Pat, his brother, and he joined us for some chestnuts with different kinds of cheese.

And red wine, for sure! Excellent red wine that is!

What a treat! What a great, friendly time!

Émissions de radio

Samedi, le 20 janvier 2013
Un client est venu acheter des marrons. Le temps était très instable. Vous avez du courage pour sortir par un temps pareil aujourd'hui! Mais il était là face à moi et dit : "Vous êtes à Radio Canada, l'émission du matin. Un auditeur nous a appelé samedi à l'émission du matin et a louangé la façon dont vous faites rôtir les marrons, la façon dont vous êtes organisé, et la façon dont vous servez vos clients. J'étais très fier de vous et de ce que vous"faites!'
Nous avons 'connecté' et avons discuté, et exprimé qui nous sommes. Je lui ai dit que c'était un grand plaisir de recevoir sa visite et les commentaires qu'il m'a donnés. A un moment, je ne pouvais plus m'exprimer, tellement mes émotions me submergeaient!...

Radio Shows!

Saturday January 20th 2013.
A customer came to buy some chestnuts. The weather was very unstable. You had to be brave to go out and face the weather today! But he was there in front of me and said:
"You were on CBC (French) radio this morning. A listener phoned into the Saturday morning show and praised the way you roast the chestnuts, the way you are set up, and the way you treat you customers. I was very proud of you and of what you are doing!"
We "connected," we talked, we expressed our views. I told him what a great pleasure his visit and his comments had given me. At a certain moment I could not talk any more as my emotions got the better of me!

Tony Greco

At every opportunity that Tony Greco has to go to "La Bottega" he stops and buys some chestnuts from me.

At every opportunity! He can be with friends, with his family, with his children and Tony stops to buy the freshly roasted chestnuts!

This morning he did so again.

Later in the day Pat Nicastro of "La Bottega" told me that: "During the radio show that Tony Greco has every Saturday, the Host told him to 'stop eating chestnuts, and.... to get on with the show!' 'I cannot stop,' answered Tony, 'I love them! They are irresistible! They are just freshly roasted, I bought them from Luciano in front of "La Bottega," on the way over! I am sorry…'".

Tony Greco hosts two radio shows every Saturday morning: "Greco Size on Team 1200" and "Greco Lean for life" on CFRA 580.

Disabled

It was cold and blowing snow, it was terrible!

She entered "La Bottega" on her wheel chair by the handicapped entrance. There was an attendant lady with her.

"Prepare me some chestnuts for when I come out! I love them! I want them! Please! Ah! The smell! I love it."

And in she went.

After a while she came out. I handed her a bag of chestnuts. She searched for her money. She did not have any.

"I'll go to the bank and I'll be right back."

"Don't worry," I said, "you can pay me another time. In this kind of weather keep warm and don't worry about the money."

The two ladies talked to each other for a few seconds. The attendant handed me $5.00 and both of them went away, happy!

Talking About Food

Here I am on a bitter cold day at the end of January 2013. The Market is almost deserted. Only a few people go by in a hurry from shelter to shelter. A customer stops, he looks like he is at ease in this cold sunny day. Fortunately there is no wind.

He buys some chestnuts and then he asks:

"Aren't you cold?"

"Actually, no." I answer. "As of now I am trying a new formula to fight the cold weather. Mario, who works at the deli counter here at 'La Bottega' has given me some delicious fresh focaccia. They make it fresh daily here. Mario puts inside it some hot red peppers with olive oil. This 'formula' works like a stove in my body. Now I know why they call them HOT peppers! They warm you up!"

So, we talk about foods and food remedies.

Garlic is a great antiseptic. The Egyptians gave a daily dose of garlic to the slave workers that built the pyramids to prevent the spread of diseases. They preserved their meat with garlic, as there were not refrigerators at that time. I personally take one little clove of garlic, that I grow myself in my back yard, every morning and every evening to combat colds.

I use locally made, unpasteurized honey that I buy here from the vendors in the Market to combat allergies, and sometime I buy and use locally made pollen that is also sold here in the Market. When in season, I buy fresh locally produced eggs. A chick, when born, does not have to eat, drink, and it is immune to any disease for 24 hours because of the antibodies that are in the eggs, thus ensuring it's health. That nourishment can surely help human beings, but we are no longer used to "natural" foods at our table!

We suffer from what I call: "The nature deficiency syndrome!"

This morning, for breakfast, I had whole wheat toast with maple syrup, goat cheese made with unpasteurized milk and, naturally, a great espresso.

The maple syrup cleans your liver. The liver is the organ that cleans our blood.

I make my own broth with chicken bones, onions, tomatoes and other vegetables. Chicken soup is considered a remedy, and the onions disinfect your blood.

Another example is here in front of us. The chestnuts! If we look at the "chestnuts nutrition facts" we notice that, among many other healthy benefits, they lower bad cholesterol, and increase good cholesterol. Furthermore they stabilize the red blood cells, and so on.

Une théorie à confirmer

Je ne l'ai pas vu pendant quelques jours, et le voici qu'il me serre la main.

"Comment allez-vous?" Je demandai.

"Je vais bien, j'étais en République Dominicaine depuis deux semaines et je suis maintenant de retour à la vie normale".

"Connaissez-vous l'une des principales raisons pour aller dans le sud l'hiver?" Je lui demandai.

"Bien, pour se détendre et profiter de la chaleur".

"Une des raisons principales est l'iode".

"L'iode?"

"Oui, l'iode qui se trouve dans l'air marin, qui est dans l'eau salée. L'iode garde la glande thyroïde en santé, qui contrôle notre métabolisme. Plutôt que d'aller dans le Sud, je mange chaque jour de la 'dulse' avec une pomme. Ici au Canada nous avons la meilleure 'dulse' au monde!"

"Dulse? Qu'est-ce que c'est?"

"La dulse est une algue marine, nous en avons de bonne qualité au Nouveau-Brunswick, dans la Baie de Fundy. L'iode est emmagasiné dans notre corps et est utilisé selon le besoin. Il est toujours bon d'avoir une réserve d'iode dans notre organisme".

Il a suivi attentivement ma présentation et il dit :

"Intéressant, je vais me souvenir de cela. Savez-vous que lorsque vous marchez à l'air froid vous respirez plus d'oxygène que quand vous respirez de l'air chaud? Parce que l'air froid est plus 'concentré' que l'air chaud. Alors, à chaque fois que vous respirez, vous inhalez plus d'oxygène".

"Je ne savais pas ça. C'est logique. Je crois que c'est une théorie qui doit être confirmée!"

A Theory to Be Confirmed

I did not see him for a few days, and there he is ready to shake hands with me.

"How are you?" I asked.

"I am fine, I was in the Dominican Republic for two weeks and now I am back to my usual life."

"Do you know one of the main reasons for going South during the winter?" I asked him.

"Well...To relax, to stay warm..."

"One of the main reason is iodine."

"Iodine?"

"Yes, iodine that is in the sea air, that is in the salt water. Iodine keeps the thyroid gland healthy and that controls our metabolism. Instead of going south I eat every day some 'dulse' with an apple. Here in Canada we have the best 'dulse' in the world!"

"Dulse? What is dulse?"

"Dulse are sea weeds, algae, we have a very good quality from New Brunswick, from the Bay of Fundy. Iodine is stored in our body and it is used when needed. It is always good to have a supply of iodine in our body."

He listened attentively my explanationand then he said:

"Interesting, I will keep this in mind. Do you know that when you walk in the cold air you breathe more oxygen than when you breathe warm air? Because cold air is more 'concentrated' than warm air. So every time you breathe you inhale more oxygen."

"I did not know that. It make sense. I believe that it is a theory that needs to be confirmed!"

Last Special Person of the Day

Some days I decide to close, and I still have some bags of chestnuts left over. I don't mind that because I take them home, I peel them and I freeze them for a later date when I need them for some special occasion or for some special recipe.

So there I am, cleaning up the burned charcoal and storing the equipment I used during the day. A man approaches me, a customer:

"How was your day... I just got back from some very good fun skating on the Canal...What a wonderful day!"

"Good for you. Would you like some chestnuts?"

"No, thank you. Besides, I have no money on me."

"Don't worry about the money. I am offering them to you..."

"No, thank you, not today..."

"You know," I said while still keeping on cleaning, "I kept this last bag for the 'Special person of the day,' and you are the one! Can I offer you these chestnuts? Please?"
He could not refuse them.

Last Special Person of the Day

It was a slow stormy day.
I decided to close early. I had one bag left. I asked myself:
"Who would be the 'special person today?'"
I had not even finished wondering when a lady stopped by.
"Do you have any chestnuts ready?"
"Yes, and I will give them to you for free!"
"No, I am going to pay you!"
I won, she took them and, while taking her hood off, she told me that she was the mother of Megan, my granddaughter's friend. What a pleasure!
Then she asked me the question that a lot of people ask:
"What do you do with the chestnuts that remain?"
"You can make chestnuts and Brussel sprouts!"
"I don't like Brussel sprouts! But I can make them with green string beans!"
"That's an idea. Try them and let me know"

Not a Coincidence

Shortly before noon, while I was roasting chestnuts, a store owner came to see me to tell me that he could smell smoke in his store. This person had mentioned this to me in the past.
I am very concerned about this, and I try everyday to do the best I can to avoid excessive smoke.
Today here he is again. I try to tell him that I am very concerned about the situation and that I try to do the best I can to avoid it, if possible. I also say that I would like to explain to him what I am doing to improve the situation.
The gentleman was firm and he reiterated once again that the smoke bothers him and his clients. I understand.
I told the gentleman:

"Maybe your building is running on negative building static pressure."

"I won't change anything in my building." He said and left.

Seated at the table next to me, near the *fornella*, was a gentleman enjoying a sandwich and other delicacies from "La Bottega."

After a few minutes I asked him what the logo on his shirt represented. He told me that he was a "Stationary Engineer," a building operator. His company designs, installs and operates building automation systems.

"This is not a coincidence." I said, "I was a building operator for 35 years. Did you listen to the conversation I had with the other gentleman?"

"Yes, I did," he said. "You were right to suggest to check the building static pressure system."

I could not believe it.

"It is not a coincidence that you are here, now. How can I quote you? My name is Luciano, what is your name?"

"Joe, I am from Rochester, New York, I am here in Ottawa for a conference on 'Stationary Engineers.' There are not too many young 'Stationary Engineers' here in Ottawa. "

"Can you please give me your business card?"

Joe looked for one but he did not have it.

"Here is mine. Please send me yours. I will ask for your comments regarding the previous conversation."

I gave Joe my business card and he will send me his.

Police Officer

Today there is the official ceremony to honor the police officers that died in the line of duty.

In downtown Ottawa there were a lot of police officers, marching bands, squadrons, and other police officers going to Parliament Hill for the "Ceremony." I had made three detours because of this. I did not mind it. It was nice to see them.

Later on in the day, while I was roasting chestnuts in front of "La Bottega," I noticed a man seated in the middle of the sidewalk pretending to be playing the guitar. He was half naked, drunk, or on drugs.

Definitely he was not in the right place. A lot of passersby had to do their utmost to avoid him. There were many people in the Market today and he was inconveniencing a lot of them. After a while a Market Ambassador, a girl, talked to him. He got up and started to walk on the sidewalk.

A few seconds later I noticed the man talking to a police office in high uniform. The officer was in Ottawa for the "Ceremony" that had just ended.

The officer was listening to the man very attentively, with great empathy and respect. The man kept talking. The officer was listening.

At a certain point when the man had concluded his arguments he appeared relieved and happy because the officer had taken the time to listen to him. He was grateful to the officer, so much so that he asked the officer for a hug.

Imagine, a drunk man, half naked, asking a police officer in high uniform to hug him!

We could see that the officer tried to hug the man but he really could not. It was too much for him. He parted from the man rather irritated and disgusted

The passersby that were watching the scene, like me, understood that the man had asked the police officer for something beyond his duty, and the officer had every right to refuse! And he did!

I still admire and respect that police officer. When he passed by me I removed my hat as a sign of respect. Maybe he did not notice it. He was probably still upset for what had happened to him.

Sono tornati

È passata qualche setimana e Gianpaolo ritorna a Ottawa per lavoro, ma questa volta con due altri colleghi. Mi dà appuntamento per sabato a mezzogiorno a "La Bottega." Ha invitato anche Paolo.

Arrivo poco prima di mezzogiorno. Entro ne "La Bottega." Penso di essere il primo arrivato. Entro ed esco così per passare il tempo. Zack mi vede, mi offre un caffè. Accetto. Me lo fa speciale come sempre. Lo bevo alla sua salute.

Alle 12:45 Paolo mi telefona, sarà in ritardo. Aspetto fuori de "La Bottega". La gente passa, mi vede, mi riconosce e chiede: "No chestnuts today?"

Un po' più tardi arriva Giampaolo con i suoi due colleghi. Entriamo ne "La Bottega" per colazione. Rocco ci accoglie con viva e sincera gioia. C'è la fila, bisogna aspettare. Rocco si assenta ed appare poco dopo con un bellissimo e ben preparato tagliere coperto di ottime fettine di pane, carciofi romani, cubetti di parmigiano, prosciutto. Irresistibile! Rocco ci offre una birra italiana, organica, non filtrata, freschissima! Il tutto rende l'attesa molto più corta.

Dopo aver pranzato, usciamo. Cosa fare? I nostri ospiti ne approfiteranno per andare a fare delle compere per la famiglia in Italia. Marco dovrebbe comperare un paio di scarpe invernali: "I Canadesi hanno una buona reputazione per le scarpe invernali." Mi dice Marco.

Colgo l'occasione per suggerirgli "Lou's Boots Store." Marco accetta. Attraversiamo la strada ed eccoci nel negozio. Riconosco il proprietario, lo presento a Marco ed esco per raggiungere gli altri. Poco dopo Marco è di ritorno con un grosso sacco. Ha trovato quello che cercava ed ha comperato un ottimo paio di scarpe invernali.

"Ti hanno trattato bene?"

"Benissimo! Mi ha anche offerto una bomboletta per renderle impermeabili!" Ci dice Marco con un grande sorriso di soddisfazione!

They Are Back!

A few weeks have gone by and Giampaolo is back in Ottawa for his work, but this time he is here with two other colleagues. He asked me to meet him Saturday at noon at "La Bottega." He has also invited Paolo.

I arrive shortly before noon. I enter "La Bottega." I think I am the first one to arrive. I enter and exit "La Bottega" to pass the time. Zack sees me and offers me an espresso. I accept. He makes it special as always! I drink it to his health.

At 12:45 Paolo calls me to tell me that he will be late. I wait outside "La Bottega." People are going by, they look at me, they recognize me, and ask:

"No chestnuts today?"

Giampaolo arrives with his two colleagues. We enter "La Bottega" for lunch. Rocco welcomes us with warmth and sincere joy. There is a line-up and we have to wait. Rocco leaves us and comes back a few minutes later with a beautiful and well prepared chopping board piled with some exquisite slices of bread, Roman artichokes, cubes of Parmesan cheese and slices of prosciutto. Irresistible!

Rocco also offer us e new Italian beer, organic, not filtered, very cold! The whole process of tasting and sampling made the waiting much shorter!

After lunch we went outside. What's next on the agenda? Our visitors will go shopping for their family in Italy. Marco wants to buy a pair of Winter boots.

"Canadians have a good reputation for Winter boots." Marco tells me.

I take the opportunity to suggest "Lou's Boots Store." Marco accepts. We cross the street and there, in the store, I recognize the owner. I introduce him to Marco and I leave to meet the others. A few minutes later Marco is back with a big bag. He had found what he was looking for. He had bought a very good pair of winter boots.

"Did they treat you well?"

"They treated me very well. They also gave me a spray bottle to make them waterproof." Marco told us with a smile of great satisfaction!

Rangers *from Toronto*

They were in Ottawa for a hockey tournament.

They were having a good time in the ByWard Market. They were very visible in their blue uniforms with the name *Rangers* written on them.

They went by me a couples of times, young, with many interests in life. I did not dare engage on any level with them. All of a sudden they stopped:

"Roasted chestnuts? I never tried one....How does it work?" pointing at the little sign that says: "Sample 25 cents."

"You see, if you want to taste one it will cost you 25 cents. You can share it with your friends so that they can acquire the taste too. It doesn't take much. If you like them then you buy them. It is like tasting wine, you take a little sip to see if you like it.

I barely finished talking and there they were, a few of them offering me the 25 cents. I told them to put it in the can, and they did.

They were very polite, they put the money gently in the can. How many quarters did they put in the can? I don't know. They were enjoying their experience.. .and my generosity. We connected very well. I liked them and we felt at ease together.

They were well-mannered in every way with me and what a positive and educational experience they were having! I was generous with them and my sincere generosity stimulated even more the dynamic of the social interaction.

What a pleasure I had! What a wonderful life experience they had…at the ByWard Market!

In Ottawa!

Un bacio…A Kiss!

She tied the leash of the cute little dog at the bike pole in front of me. She was young, colourfully dressed, with a certain flair… I liked it.

She smiled at me while entering "La Bottega."

"Don't worry. I will look after your cute little pet. I have been dog- sitting, grocery sitting, husband, boyfriend, girlfriend- sitting. You can trust me!."

I kept roasting chestnuts and serving my customers.

A family came. I served them. They looked at the dog and found it very cute.

"Who's is it?"

"A lady who just went inside and I am sitting it." I said with a brief smile. They approached the dog who responded to them immediately.The young lady came out and witnessed the happiness that the little dog was creating. Before going to the dog she came to me and she gave me a …*bacio*….*Perugina*, one of those chocolate kisses…I could not resist. I gave her two kisses on her cheeks.

For a second the family watched us. They liked the exchange. They smiled at us.

Venditore di sogni

Franco Junior è appena arrivato a Ottawa per affari. Si tratterrà solo qualche giorno. Mi sorprende che, appena arrivato, sia venuto a trovarmi mentre sono al Mercato ad arrostire castagne. Dopo i doverosi saluti di "ben tornato a Ottawa," Franco rimane là a guardare come esercito la professione di castagnaro e soprattutto come interagisco con i clienti. Tra un cliente e l'altro parliamo, ci informiamo a vicenda, ma Franco continua a guardare.

"Vedo che hai delle esperienze fantastiche da condividere," mi dice ad un certo momento. "Credo che posso senz'altro definirti un 'venditore di sogni.' Sei un leader delle emozioni!"

"Grazie per l'incoraggiamento," rispondo. "In questi giorni sto pensando di scrivere *Le cronache dell'amante di castagne* e penso che citerò anche te e questa esperienza che stiamo vivendo ora. Come vuoi che ti chiami nel libro?"

"Chiamami Franco Junior, per me va benissimo!"

A Salesman of Dreams

Franco Junior has just arrived in Ottawa for business. He will stay here only a few days. He has just arrived and has surprised me at the Market while I am roasting chestnuts.

After the very joyous greetingand a warm "welcome back to Ottawa!" Franco stays there near me, watching while I carry onwith my business of roasting chestnuts. More than anything also, he watches how I interact with the customers. Between clients we talk, we exchange information. Meanwhile Franco continues watching me.

"I see that you have some fantastic experiences to share" he tells me. "I can certainly call you a dream salesman and a leader of emotions!"

"I thank you for the praise." I answer. "Lately I am considering writing the *Chronicles of a Chestnut Lover* and I think I will mention you and this experience that we are living now. How should I call you in the book?"

"Call me Franco Junior, for me that is fine."

"The Salt of the Earth"

She approached me with curiousity.

"Roasted chestnuts?"

"Yes. Sample one."

"Thank you. It is delicious!"

And we started to talk, to chat. Nanette, that's her name, told me that she was going to turn 71 soon and that she was not seeing a bright future for the young generation.

"Too many things going wrong. I am very afraid for them!"

"What you feel is normal," I said to Nanette. "When Goya, a famous Spanish artist, reached a certain age, he painted the whole house where he lived in a dark olive green color. In the painting there were two men, deep to their waste, in quicksand. They both were sinking, and yet they were beating each other. They both knew they were going to die, and yet they were fighting each other to death.

"That is what I call human irrationality. It will never change! It will get worse and worse!

"We will never learn from history. But," I kept talking, "Goya changed to a more positive philosophy of life thanks to 'La Latiera de Bordeaux,' a little girl that was bringing him milk every day to his house. He did a beautiful painting of her, one of his best, and one of his last."

Nanette was listening to me very attentively. Maybe I was able to alleviate her feeling about human irrationality.

"You are the salt of the earth!" She said before she left.

Three Swiss Girls

Giovanni is "the cheese expert" at "La Bottega." This morning, a very cold morning, I see him across the street, by the Market building talking to three girls. When he crossed the street I told him:

"They could not resist your charm!"

Giovanni, indeed, has a very nice distinct personality.

"No," he said, "they are three very nice and beautiful Swiss girls who were looking for the nearest Starbuck Cafe. I had difficulty understanding them. If they come around give them some chestnuts. I will pay you!".

Great Emotions

A group of seven people came toward me while I was roasting chestnuts. It looked like it was composed of three family generations: grandparents, parents, children. "The mother" was helping the "grandfather" because he had difficulty walking. While they were approaching they were talking. I could distinguish only the word "castanas...castanas" or something like it, in their sentences. They came near me, the mother, the guide, started explaining to the other members of the family, the way I was roasting the chestnuts. She asked me, in English, to show the burning charcoal to her family members.

During all this time I was drawn to the elderly man, the grandfather. I could feel that he really wanted to try a "freshly roasted chestnut" and, even before all the questions were answered, in a fraction of a second I took a chestnut, wrapped it in a napkin and I gave it to the lady-guide. With a gesture I let her know that it was for the grandfather.

What a surprise! The man looked at me with unexplainable gratitude as if I had fulfilled a dream. A beautiful dream!

The lady peeled the chestnut, split it and put a piece in his mouth. The man could not do it himself. He was disabled. Here he is in front of me savouring the chestnut and reminiscing who knows what great sensations, great feelings... dreams... Who knows!

The whole experience was very intense, emotional and very important for all of us standing around the *fornella*. With the smell of roasted chestnuts we could feel a strong bond of friendship and love among all of us.

What an experience!

Back to reality.

The grandmother signaled to me that he, the grandfather, was her husband. The lady guide introduced me to the whole family. I offered them some samples.

"No, thank you. We are going to buy some."

I served them.

Once they were ready to leave me, very happy for their experience, I asked them:

"Where are you from?"

"We are Palestinians."

I really hope they will be back to share again another beautiful human experience!

Canadian Museum of Civilizations

I went to a round table discussion at the Canadian Museum of Civilization because of the proposed changes: a new name and a new mandate for this highly respected and very popular Canadian institution of which I have been a member for many years.

After the round table, that I found very well organized, very informative and educational, I struck up a conversation with one of the ladies who was seated at our table. Naturally...I talked about... guess what?

Chestnuts!

I told the lady what you, the reader of these chronicles, already knows. But this time I told her about the turkey stuffing.

Don't forget that this chronicle happened in a museum.

Back in the 1600 the Pilgrims came to the American continent with the *Mayflower* that subsequently sank. They were saved from starvation by the aboriginal people. The aboriginal women in their cooking used stuffing made of meat, fish, wild rice and corn.

At that time, on the American continent, there were four billion chestnuts trees, and a multitude of wild turkeys.

While I was studying this historic chapter, I put two and two together: turkeys, chestnuts and the aboriginal women that were using all sorts of meats for stuffing. Why not turkeys stuffed with chestnuts?

I told this theory of mine to a gentleman, one of my customers in the Market and he, to my great surprise, told me:

"You are right! The Aboriginals were eating wild turkeys stuffed with chestnuts!"

He also told me that he was a Museum historian.

The lady was fascinated by my story and the location in

which I told her... the Grand Hall of the Museum of Civilization where the Canadian Aboriginal culture is alive and well. One of the most beautiful Museum in the world! What an impact! Ever since I started to promote the "chestnut culture" my daughter has created a very good recipe for "chestnut turkey stuffing!"

Il tuo gesto basta

Arrivano da Montreal. Sono due venditori. Si avvicinano.
"Caldarroste! Che meraviglia!"
Vannno alla macchina e ritornano con le mani piene di campioni di prodotti alimentari. Apro loro la porta de "La Bottega."
Appena ho arrostito le prime castagne ne faccio dei sachetti e li porto al personale della cucina de "La Bottega," a Raymond a Pat Nicastro, ed un sachetto ai due rappresentanti di Montreal che, sorpresi, mi ringraziano.
Ritorno alla fornella.
Dopo qualche tempo eccoli qua i due rappresentanti.
Uno di loro mi porge un vasetto di peperoncini piccanti sott'olio d'oliva.
"Ti prego, per ora prendi questo vasetto, ti prometto che ti porterò un vasetto di crema di tartufo, una nostra specialità."
Non so cosa dire. Questa persona ha apprezzato talmente il mio gesto che non sa proprio come ringraziarmi.
"Carissimo. Il tuo gesto mi basta. Ho capito quanto voi avete apprezzato il mio. Il vasetto dei peperoncini mi basta."
"Grazie ancora, ti lascierò una piccola sorpresa qua con Pat nostro amico, la prossima volta che saremo a Ottawa! Ciao."

Your Gesture Is Enough

They are from Montreal. They are two salesmen. They approached me.
"Roasted chestnuts! How marvelous!"
They return to the car. They come back with their hands full of grocery samples. I open the door for them as they enter "La Bottega."

As soon as I roast the first chestnuts I make some bags and I bring them to the personnel of the kitchen of "La Bottega," to Raymond, to Pat Nicastro, and one bag for the two salesmen from Montreal. I surprise them! They thank me.

I go back to the *fornella.*

After a little while there they are, the two salesmen.

One of them offers me a jar of hot red pepper in olive oil.

"Please take this jar, I promise I will bring you a jar of cream of tartufo. It's the specialty of our House!"

I do not know what to say. These people appreciated my gesture so much that....they didn't know how to thank me!

"My dear. Your act of giving is enough for me. I understand that you appreciated mine. The hot pepper jar is enough for me."

"I thank you again. I will leave a surprise for you with our friend Pat next time you come to Ottawa."

You Italians!

He was passing by. He stoppped.

"Roasted chestnuts? I will buy some."

I gave him a bag of roasted chestnuts. He paid me. He opened the bag and started to peel and eat the freshly roasted chestnuts right there in front of me.

I kept doing what I was doing.

"You Italians make the greatest food and the greatest sports-cars!"

He stated and then he left.

The Toonie

She was young and very gracious. She filled the electric chair were she was seated. She approached the *fornella*.

"Do you know where the bead store is?" She asked me.

I stopped my work and pointed towards the bead store. She was very happy.

"Wait a minute. I said, "I have a map of the Market. Here it is. Keep it for future reference."

I always keep some maps of the ByWard Market with me so that I can give them to the tourists visiting Ottawa.

"Oh, thank you. I really appreciate it. How much do I owe you?"

"Don't worry. You don't owe me anything. Enjoy your day."

"Here, take this." She handed me a toonie.

"No, no, it's OK. Keep it." I said.

She insisted. I "had" to take the toonie!

A toonie that I could not spend to buy any "material things" a toonie that for me had a priceless value.

I gave that toonie to charity.

The Loonie

She comes by every day when I am in the Market. She has a light violet coat always open even on bitter cold days. Today was a nice warm day and she was dressed in a light dress. She approached me, as usual, singing an Italian song. She likes singing. After the song she told me that she had some financial problems. We chat.

I offer her some freshly roasted chestnuts. She wants only one, not any one! That one!

She points at one perfectly roasted. I give it to her wrapped in a napkin. She thanks me with a sincere smile.

Then, to my great surprise, she hands me a loonie.

I indicated to her to put it in the can were the spare change is. "Not this one. It is too shiny! This is a lucky loonie. Keep it for yourself. It will bring you good luck!" It was Thanksgiving. I put the loonie in my pocket. When I arrived home I gave that "special loonie" to my granddaughter.

Pair of Boots

She stopped for some freshly roasted chestnuts. She was wearing a nice, orange and elegant hat. I was serving her but at my right another lady wanted a sample. I looked at the first customer and she nodded and allowed me to serve her. I served her a sample. While I was serving her I noticed her swollen hands. She appeared "different", took the sample, thanked me and left. I then served the other lady, the elegant one, with the orange hat.

The day went by. Later I saw once again the lady with the orange hat coming toward me. She approached me and asked if I would see the other lady again.

"I don't know, I don't think I will" I said.

"If you see her again give her this pair of boots." And she handed me a bag with a pair of boots in it.

I thanked her and she thanked me!

* * *

There she is, always dressed the same, I gave her a chestnut.

"I can not pay you I am having financial problems! Those people should be sent to another planet." She said.

I could not have agreed more!

I looked at her, at her feet. She was wearing a pair of those croc-like plastic sandals, without socks! It was bitterly cold and windy!

"I bought these 'shoes' at Dollarama for $2 !" She said.

"Here, I have a pair of good boots for you, try them on." She tried them on.

"They are a bit too big."

"They will be just fine when you put a pair of good wool socks on with those boots."

"Yes! I have wool socks at home, I will be by tomorrow and show you that I wear the boots and the socks"

* * *

Today the elegant lady with the orange hat came by with her husband, they were carrying a few bags of clothing.
"Here. I leave them with you, please give them to her."
I could not refuse them. I really hoped that "the other " lady would pass by.
And indeed she did to my great satisfaction. Was it a miracle?
She smelled of alcohol and her hands were cold and swollen. She was carrying a bag with some empty paper cups.
"I am very happy to see you. Look what I have for you. Some nice and very warm clothing that will help you stay warm during the winter! Look at this, and this, and this...The lady that gave them to me is just like you! They will fit you perfectly! Next time you come by I want to see you well and warmly dressed."
"You remind me of my father. He was so caring. I will use them for sure. Thank you!"
I helped her carry all the bags, 6 or 7of them, and then she left.

I really hope she will be back next week, well- dressed and without the smell of alcohol.

Chronicles from Alberta

They stopped by, two very charming ladies, one more so than the other. I served them a sample of freshly roasted chestnuts. They loved it!
They bought a bag. We talked and I told them about the "Chestnuts culture ... the social interaction ... about the book I am writing....
They were from Alberta. They were in Ottawa for a Conference about community. What a great topic! I loved it. We continued to converse....
We interacted so well that one of them took a photo of me and the other lady.
Another photo with the two of us closer.

"That's a very nice photo. I will send it to you with my chronicles!"

She asked me for my business card. I could not refuse her. She was too charming!

Appendix

ceuces with him.

"Make a wish," he tells them as they slip the warm packages into their pockets.

Luciano's first experience with roasted chestnuts occurred more than 60 years ago, in the Italian village of Vittorio Veneto, north of Venice, where he grew up. There was no central heating, he recalls, and so his mother, widowed by the Second World War's Russian front when Luciano was just a baby, would be up early, cooking on the stove.

He remembers, too, always wearing shorts, even on cold days. The war had just ended, and they had no money for long pants, and when he left for school, his mother would hand him chestnuts to put in his pockets.

"That was my breakfast," he says, "and

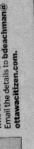

African, South American — they know about chestnuts, and they love them."

And with his government pension and modest lifestyle, he admits he doesn't rely on his income from selling chestnuts.

"But when you give a child warm chestnuts to put in his pocket, and you see his face light up, to me there is no price for that.

"Freshly roasted chestnuts ... what do you need more than that in life?"

Through profiles here and online, Bruce Deachman uncovers the people who bring Ottawa to life; people who exhibit an unusual passion or obsession. Do you know someone who is one in a million? A friend who keeps pigeons? A neice who does nothing but enter contests? Email the details to **bdeachman@ottawacitizen.com.**

PIERRE JURY SAVEUR   pjury@ledroit.com

Renaissance de la châtaigne rôtie

À moins qu'ils n'aient vécu quelques années en Europe, les Nord-Américains ignorent pas mal tout des châtaignes. C'est qu'ici, une maladie a littéralement décimé, aux États-Unis du moins, au début du XXᵉ siècle, les quelque 4 milliards de châtaigniers qui se retrouvaient surtout au sud, mais aussi sur la côte est du pays.

Malgré des efforts bien présent, quoiqu'un peu vu marqués de repro-plantation, a par-tega Nicastro, sur le marché By, et participe à divers événements comme l'ouverture de la Vendemmia, la fête des vendanges dans la Petite Italie.

Depuis deux saisons, Luciano Pradal a repris à Ottawa la préparation ancestrale de châtaigne rôtie. Il se tient devant l'épicerie italienne La Bottega Nicastro...

De retour

Mais n'ayez crainte, M. Pradal se promène bien d'être là maintenant...

Le pain des pauvres

« Vous voulez goûter à une châtaigne rôtie ? », lance-t-il à tous...

Soul contre tous, armé que d'un gril de fortune qu'un ami lui a confectionné, Luciano Pradal brave l'hiver pour offrir aux gens de la région et aux touristes de passage divers châtaignes fraîchement récoltées...

offrir une châtaigne. Un geste tout simple d'humanisme.

2010 Winterganes

Today is Thursday January 14, 2010

Fresh, toasty chestnuts to appear on the streets of Ottawa

By ronaele Wed, Jan 13 2010 Ottawa's Ottawa Run, Paul's section of Food, Drink and Dining in the Capital

JAN 13 10 - 6:15 PM — Even as a wee lad of about six or seven, I finally recall the days when mum and dad would meet up with friends and a gaggle of us kiddos in tow to shop for Christmas presents at Honest Ed's on Bloor Street, near Bathurst in downtown Toronto. It was always a fabulous outing, one we eagerly anticipated not only because shopping at Honest Ed's was like going to a party, but because we knew dad would stop by a street vendor afterward to buy us kids a bag (or two, or three) of fresh piping-hot chestnuts from a sidewalk vendor.

"Last year I went to Milano to a conference on tourism and saw this guy roasting chestnuts in a *fornella*, which is basically a small oven on a cart fired by lump hardwood charcoal," Luciano says. "So I took some photos of this operation and gave them to John Frigo of Venice Steel Works on Larch Street, here in Ottawa, and he fabricated a prototype oven and cart."

The oven consists of a 24-inch-diameter firebox to contain the glowing charcoal, a perforated round tray to roast the chestnuts that pivots on top, and a smaller tray above the roasting chamber to keep the finished nuts toasty warm. It takes about 10 minutes to roast each batch of chestnuts, which are imported from Italy through La Bottega in the ByWard Market.

"The oven is fantastic," says Pat Nicastro, owner of La Bottega.

"It's the first time I've seen it in Ottawa. You see them in every European city and they're wonderful."

Luciano already has city health department and bylaw enforcement approval to sell in the ByWard Market, says Paolo Copelli, markets co-ordinator for the City of Ottawa, who cannot recall anyone selling street chestnuts in Ottawa until now.

But the entrepreneur plans to start small, giving away free samples this Friday, Saturday and Sunday outside Pasticceria Gelateria Italiana at 200 Preston St. from 11 a.m. to 4 p.m.

After that, he'll be selling roasted chestnuts at $5 for about a dozen on Jan. 21 to 24 from his stand outside La Bottega, 64 George St., from 11 a.m. to 4 p.m. The following weekend, he'll be outside Casa Nicastro on Preston Street. For a current rundown on where he will be and times, call Pasticceria Gelateria Italiana at 613-233-2104 until he gets a schedule posted on the internet.

Investors in the fledgling project are Luciano, John, and Joe Calabro (*L-R in photo, left*) of Pasticceria Gelateria Italiana.

"We think it just adds to the market uniqueness," Paolo says. "It has flavour and character and it makes the market that much more vibrant."

If the pilot project succeeds, Luciano hopes one day to operate as many as six sidewalk chestnut carts at various locations through the city. The chestnut season typically runs from late autumn to about March — perfect sweet sustenance to sustain the soul after hopping from store to store or enjoying a bracing skate on the canal.

Now, many years later than I care to count, I've often wondered why chestnut vendors never made an appearance in Ottawa. It always seemed a bit odd to me, given that roasted chestnuts are an Italian tradition and, we all know, Ottawa has a proud and vibrant Italian community that contributes so much to our social, cultural and culinary fabric.

Where are the chestnut vendors in the nation's capital, you may ask?

The really great news, they are coming. This week, in fact.

John estimates the prototype cart costs about $1,000 in material, not counting labour to fabricate the steel that could add another $2,500 to the price.

"If there's a market for this then there's the possibility of a half-dozen carts in the future selling chestnuts from about October to April," Joe says.

"We've been talking about this idea for about a year, and basically it just took off. We'll be at different spots each week," Calabro says.

The chestnuts are very environmentally friendly, as shells are completely compostable. The treats are sold without additives, salt or sugar.

"It's all natural," Luciano says.

Yes, Ottawa is getting a winter taste of sweet roasted Italian chestnuts being sold on the street. Barely for the first time by an outdoor food vendor.

Freshly roasted chestnuts have long been a sidewalk winter tradition in Italy and in larger North American cities like New York and Toronto. But until now, no one can recall chestnuts making an appearance on Ottawa sidewalks — certainly not in recent memory.

Naturally good, that is.

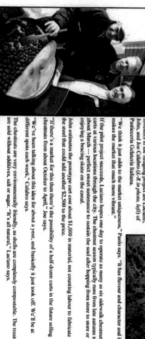

(*Photos by Pat McGrath, Ottawa Citizen*)

Entrepreneurs wheel out roasted Italian chestnuts

BY RON EADE

Ottawa is getting a winter taste of sweet roasted Italian chestnuts being sold for the first time by an outdoor street food vendor.

Freshly roasted chestnuts have long been a sidewalk winter tradition in Italy and in larger North American cities like New York and Toronto. But until now, no one can recall chestnuts making an appearance on Ottawa sidewalks — certainly not in recent memory.

Luciano Pradal, a retired commercial building maintenance operator who immigrated to Canada from northern Italy in 1966, was inspired a year ago to introduce street-roasted chestnuts to the nation's capital as a cultural experience.

"Last year I went to Milano to a conference on tourism and saw this guy roasting chestnuts in a formelli, which is basically a small oven on a cart fired by lump hardwood charcoal," Pradal says.

"So I took some photos of his operation and gave them to John Frigo of Vecsic Steel Works on Larch Street, here in Ottawa, and he fabricated a prototype oven and cart."

The oven on the metal cart consists of a 24-inch-diameter firebox to contain the glowing charcoal, a perforated round tray to roast the chestnuts that pivots on top, and a smaller tray above the roasting chamber to keep the finished nuts toasty warm. It

takes about 10 minutes to roast each batch of chestnuts, which are imported from Italy through La Bottega in the ByWard Market.

"The oven is fantastic," says Pat Nicastro, owner of La Bottega.

"It's the first time I've seen it in Ottawa. You see them in every European city and they're wonderful."

'You see them in every European city and they're wonderful!'

PAT NICASTRO, owner of La Bottega, on the chestnut cart

But the entrepreneur plans to start small, giving away free samples Friday, Saturday and Sunday outside Pasticceria Gelateria Italiana at 200 Preston St. from 11 a.m. to 4 p.m.

After that, he'll be selling roasted chestnuts at $5 for about a dozen on Jan. 21 to 24 from his stand outside La Bottega, 64 George St., from 11 a.m. to 4 p.m. The following weekend, he'll be outside Casa Nicastro on Preston Street.

Pradal already has city health department and bylaw enforcement approval to sell in the ByWard Market, says Paolo Copelli, markets coverdinator for the City of Ottawa, who cannot recall anyone selling street chestnuts in Ottawa until now.

Frigo estimates the prototype cart cost about $1,000 in material, not counting labour to fabricate the steel that could add another $2,500 to the price.

"If there's a market for this then there's the possibility of a half-dozen carts in the future selling chestnut from about October to April," Calabro says.

"We've been talking about this idea for about a year, and basically it just took off. We'll be at different spots each week," Calabro says.

The chestnuts are very environmentally friendly, as shells are completely compostable. The treats are sold without any additives, salt or sugar. "It's all natural," Pradal says.

For a current rundown on where he will be and times, call Pasticceria Gelateria Italiana at 613-235-2104 until he gets a schedule posted on the Internet.

Investors in the fledgling project are Fred Frigo, and Joe Calabro of Pasticceria Gelateria Italiana.

"We think it just adds to the market uniqueness," Paolo says.

"It has flavour and character and it makes the market that much more vibrant."

If the pilot project succeeds, Pradal hopes one day to operate as many as six sidewalk chestnut carts at various locations through the city.

The chestnut season typically runs from late autumn to about March — perfect sweet sustenance to warm the soul after hopping between stores or enjoying a bracing winter skate on the canal.

Luciano Pradal hoists a sample from Ottawa's first street-vending chestnut cart.

Chestnuts nutrition facts

Richly flavored, starchy, chestnuts are popular cool season edible nuts of northern hemisphere. The nuts are native to hilly forest of China, Japan, Europe, and North America. Botanically they belong to the **beech** or *fagaceae* family of the genus: **Castenea**.

Castanea are very large deciduous trees. They are monoecious, bearing both male and female flowers ("catkins"), in the same tree. Castaneas have a remarkable history to narrate. The once mighty American chestnut trees were mostly wiped out by chestnut blight (Cryphonectria parasitica) early in the 20th century. renewed interest has been growing to revive the native chestnut trees in the whole of USA.

Once pollinated, female flowers develop in to large spiny burr or involucres enclosing 2-3 nuts. The fruit is quite large in size compared to its peers like cashews, macadamia etc. Each nut features smooth, glossy dark brown color outer shell, 1-1.5 inch in diameter and weighing 8-12 g depending up on the species. Inside they have creamy white, sweet and starchy kernel.

Four main species of chestnut trees are being cultivated worldwide for their nuts; **Castanea sativa** in Europe, **C. dentata** in North America, **C.mollissima** in china and **C. crenata** in Japan. United States is the main importer of chest nuts from European Union, although china has been the largest exporter of nuts worldwide, especially to Japan.

Health benefits of chestnut

- Chestnuts, unlike other nuts and seeds, are relatively **low in calories**; contain less fat but are rich in minerals, vitamins and phyto-nutrients that benefit health.

- Nutritionally, chestnuts are similar to other starchy foods such as sweet potato, sweet corn, potatoes etc consisting of mainly starch. However, they also contain high quality proteins.

- They are good source of **dietary fiber**; provides 8.1 g (about 21% of RDI) per 100 g. Fiber diet helps lower blood cholesterol levels by remove excess cholesterol absorbing in the intestines.

- Chestnuts stand out from other nuts and seeds because of their nutrition contents. They are exceptionally rich in **vitamin-C**. 100 g nuts provide 43 mg of vitamin C (72 % of DRI). Vitamin C is essential for formation of matrix in teeth, bones and blood vessels. Being a strong anti-oxidant, it offers protection from harmful free radicals.

- They are the one of the nuts rich in **folates**. 100 g nuts provide 62 mg of folates (or 15.5%). Folic acid is required for the formation of red blood cells, DNA synthesis. Adequate consumption of food rich in folates during peri-conception period helps prevent neural tube defects in the fetus.

- They are rich source of mono-unsaturated fatty like **oleic acid** (18:1) and **palmitoleic acids** (16:1). Studies suggest that monounsaturated fats in the diet help lower total as well as LDL (bad cholesterol) and increase HDL (good cholesterol) levels in the blood. Mediterranean diet which is rich in dietary fiber, monounsaturated fatty acids, omega fatty acids and antioxidants help prevent coronary artery disease and strokes by favoring healthy blood lipid profile.

- The nuts are excellent source of **minerals** such as iron, calcium, potassium, magnesium, manganese, phosphorus and zinc. Provide very good amount of potassium (518 mcg / 100 g). Potassium helps counter hypertensive action of sodium, lowers heart rate and blood pressure. Iron helps prevent microcytic-anemia. Magnesium and phosphorus are important components of bone metabolism.

- They are also rich in many important B-complex groups of vitamins. 100 g of nuts provide 11% of niacin, 29% of pyridoxine (vit.B-6), 100% of thiamin, and 12% of riboflavin.

- Chestnuts, like hazelnuts and almonds, are free in gluten and therefore popular ingredient in the preparation of gluten free food formulas for gluten-sensitive, wheat allergy and celiac disease persons.

- Chinese nuts (C.mollissima) are good in vitamin A; provide 202 IU per 100 g.

Selection and storage

Chestnuts are cool season crop, begin available in the markets from October through March, peaking in December. In Asia and Europe they are still harvested and processed by traditional methods.

In the stores, choose big sized, fresh nuts. Since they are rich in starch and fewer fats than most other nuts, they tend to spoil rather quickly if exposed to air and less humid conditions for longer period. To verify freshness, cut open some sample nuts and check for heavy, meaty, creamy white kernel inside since often-times it is difficult to find out damaged nuts by their outer appearance. Avoid nuts with greenish mold developed between the convoluted folds and the nut kernel and its outer shell.

Chestnuts should be treated more like vegetables and fruits than nuts whe it comes to their storage. Once at home; they sooner packed and kept in cold storage in the refrigerator, set with high relative humidity where they remain fresh for few weeks.

Preparation and serving methods

Chestnuts are savored for centuries by native Americans as their staple foods, used like modern day potatoes. The nuts are very sweet and flavorful.

Here are some serving tips:

- They can be eaten raw, boiled or by roasting. To roast, small incisions made over dome side of the nuts to prevent busting.

See the table below for in depth analysis of nutrients:

Chestnuts, European, raw, unpeeled (Castanea sativa).
Nutritional value per 100 g.
(Source: USDA National Nutrient data base)

Principle	Nutrient Value	Percentage of RDA
Energy	213 Kcal	11%
Carbohydrates	45.54 g	35%
Protein	2.42 g	4%
Total Fat	2.26 g	10%
Cholesterol	0 mg	0%
Dietary Fiber	8.1 g	21%
Vitamins		
Folates	62 mcg	15.5%
Niacin	1.179 mg	7%
Pantothenic acid	0.309 mg	11%
Pyridoxine	0.376 mg	29%
Riboflavin	0.168 mg	13%
Thiamin	0.238 mg	20%
Vitamin A	28 IU	1%
Vitamin C	43 mg	72%
Electrolytes		
Sodium	3 mg	0%
Potassium	518 mg	11%
Minerals		
Calcium	27 mg	3%
Copper	0.447 mg	50%
Iron	1.01 mg	13%
Magnesium	32 mg	8%
Manganese	0.952 mg	41%
Phosphorus	93 mg	19%
Zinc	0.52 mg	5%
Phyto-nutrients		
Phyto-sterols	22 mcg	--

- The nuts are used as main ingredient in poultry stuffing, especially in thanksgiving turkey.

- Chestnut flour is also favored in many **Tuscany recipes** such as polenta, sweet breads, biscuits, cakes, soups and ice-cream.

- **Marron glace** is extremely popular in Europe where large sized, high quality European chestnuts (marrone di lucerna) used. To prepare marron glace or glazed chestnuts, the nuts are soaked in water and then dipped and heated in gradual concentration of sugar vanilla syrup for several days and then dried.

- They are also used to make chestnut butter-cream.

THE SOCIETY OF ONTARIO NUT GROWERS

SONG was established in 1972 with the following objectives:

1 - To promote interest in nut bearing plants, their products and their culture.

2 - To promote research in the breeding and culture of nut bearing plants suited to Ontario conditions.

3 - To encourage planting of improved cultivars in gardens and orchards, on farms and public lands.

4 - To disseminate information on propagation techniques and cultural practices.

5 - To provide opportunities for closer association among nut growers residing in Ontario.

ACTIVITIES:

The Society of Ontario nut Growers has four meetings per year.

The **spring meeting** is usually an auction held in or near Toronto.

The **summer meeting** is usually a business meeting with presentations on nut growing and/or a tour of nut trees.

The **fall meeting** is a tour of a special nut planting and often an exchange of nuts and seed.

The **winter meeting** is a technical meeting where a day of speakers are arranged on timely nut growing subjects.

The *SONGNEWS* bulletin is issued three, sometimes four times each year with timely articles on nut growing and related information.

Three year new memberships receive a free copy of *NUT TREE ONTARIO, A PRACTICAL GUIDE*. SONG's 127 page nut tree manual to get them started.

SONG MEMBERSHIP FORM

Name:_____   Date:_____

Address:_____City/Prov/St_____Postal/Zip_____

Telephone: _____ ☐ I wish to receive email newsletters

Renewal: ☐   New Membership ☐ Email: _____

Payment enclosed for: ☐ 1 Year $17.00   ☐ 3 Years $45.00

☐ Please send my free copy of *NUT TREE ONTARIO, A PRACTICAL GUIDE* with my NEW 3 year membership.

☐ I wish to buy *NUT TREE ONTARIO, A PRACTICAL GUIDE* and I enclose $24.00 including postage

☐ I wish to buy **NUT GROWING ONTARIO STYLE, SONG'S** former handbook. I enclose $16 includes postage.

Send to: SONG, Ernie Grimo -Treasurer, R.R. 3, Niagara-on-the-Lake. Ont. L0S 1J0. Make cheques payable to SONG. Your cancelled cheque is your receipt.

The

Canadian Sweet Chestnut

- Journal of the Canadian Chestnut Council

Issue # 60   March, 2013

http://www.canadianchestnutcouncil.org

In this issue: - Meet the New Director, Summary of Executive and Fund-Raising Meetings, Recent communications, CCC supporters and Donors.

Meet the New Director, Christine Vey

Christine has volunteered with the CCC at Onondaga Farms for the past 2 years and became an official Director at the 2012 AGM. She feels at home in a pick-up truck, on a tractor, leading a tour or with a shovel in her hand planting chestnuts. She has proven to be great addition to the CCC executive with positive suggestions and creative ideas and is a member of the new Fund Raising Committee. Welcome to the CCC. Her biography, in Christine's words, is as follows:

I was born and raised in Brantford, Ontario. Attended Conestoga College in the Recreation Leadership Program. Started at Bronte Creek Provincial Park after college, and worked there for 7 years as a Farm Assistant. After taking maternity leave, I found a position at Tim Horton Onondaga Farms, working with youth (running programs that were agriculture-based) and also on the farm. Working in a variety of different roles, I have been with Onondaga Farms now for almost 8 years. It has been an absolute pleasure working for this organization and being a part of the amazing things that happen every day! Currently I share the Farm Manager position with John Hill, and together we provide opportunities for children and adults to experience farm life, in a safe and accepting environment. With the large chestnut plantation on property (started by John Hill and Gil Henderson), it was a natural fit to learn more and become involved in the Canadian Chestnut Council. I look forward to learning more from the existing members and to help bring back this beautiful tree.

Christine Vey became a Director at the 2012 AGM. She is active in the Fundraising Committee and works full time at THF/Onondaga Farms.

Correspondence: Keith, a new member from New Brunswick, has requested information on locations of native chestnuts in that province. He has a chestnut leaf from a leaf collection that his father-in-law made while attending the University of New Brunswick in the '50s. His father-in-law feels that the tree must have been in the Fredericton area because of difficulties with transportation at that time. Jocelyn Clark, our Honorary Member from down east, is assisting him with tree locations in Nova Scotia but doesn't have information on New Brunswick. If anyone has information on American chestnut, native or planted in New Brunswick, please let myself or Jocelyn know and we will pass along the information. It may be coincidental but in the recent Jan/Feb issue of the Journal of the American Chestnut Foundation, there is an article on a